423.1
D794

What's Up?

A Guide to American

CollegeSpeak

Slang & Idioms for TOEFL® Students

KGL

Jamie Drucker

THOMSON

PETERSON'S

Australia • Canada • Mexico • Singapore • Spain • United Kingdom • United States

THOMSON
PETERSON'S

About The Thomson Corporation and Peterson's

With revenues of US$7.8 billion, The Thomson Corporation (www.thomson.com) is a leading global provider of integrated information solutions for business, education, and professional customers. Its Learning businesses and brands (www.thomsonlearning.com) serve the needs of individuals, learning institutions, and corporations with products and services for both traditional and distributed learning.

Peterson's, part of The Thomson Corporation, is one of the nation's most respected providers of lifelong learning online resources, software, reference guides, and books. The Education Supersite^{SM} at www.petersons.com—the Internet's most heavily traveled education resource—has searchable databases and interactive tools for contacting U.S.-accredited institutions and programs. In addition, Peterson's serves more than 105 million education consumers annually.

Acknowledgments
For my sister, Mandie Rosenberg, the true author of the family.
And thanks to my classmates, colleagues, and students for speaking so "improperly."

For more information, contact Peterson's, 2000 Lenox Drive, Lawrenceville, NJ 08648; 800-338-3282; or find us on the World Wide Web at www.petersons.com/about.

ISBN 0-7689-1243-1

Printed in Canada

10 9 8 7 6 5 4 3 2 1   05 04 03

Contents

Introduction

Welcome to college! This is the beginning of an exciting time in your life, but it can also be a challenging time. College students leave home, often for the first time, and find themselves in a strange environment. But if college life is unfamiliar to an American student studying at an American university, it is even more unfamiliar to you. You not only have to adjust to college life, you must also adjust to life in a new country!

Part of adjusting to life in a new country is learning the language. You've already done so, because you are studying for the TOEFL or have been accepted into an American college or university. But the language you mastered for the TOEFL does not include slang and may only include basic idioms. (Remember: **Slang** is the use of colorful and informal words in casual speech, and **idioms** are phrases that have nonliteral meanings.)

Teenagers and college students are notorious for their use of slang. Slang is a way for young adults to differentiate themselves from their parents' generation. In fact, many parents don't even understand half of the stuff their kids say! And slang is ever-changing. New slang terms are invented every day. This book includes slang and idioms that are fairly common, but note that each group of friends may have its own slang terms that people outside their group may not understand.

The purpose of this book is not to supply you with words that you can use to sound "cool." Instead, we want you to get familiar with the language you'll hear in real-life college situations. This book doesn't contain *every* slang term in the English language; otherwise, it would be thousands of pages long! But we have offered you what we believe is a solid sampling of terms to get you started.

Have fun!

How to Use This Book

The words in this guide are categorized by subject. However, you will find that many words can easily fit in more than one category. For instance, the word *hottie* (an attractive person) appears in Chapter 8, which is about dating and romance. However, because *hottie* is a word that describes a person, it could easily fit into Chapter 6, which is about types of people and emotions.

Points to keep in mind:

- The *part of speech* is included for each term in the book. The abbreviations are as follows:

    n   noun

    v   verb or verb phrase

    adj   adjective

    adv   adverb

- Following each definition is a sentence or short conversation that is an example of how you would hear the term used in common speech.

- Words or phrases within the definitions may be <u>underlined</u>. This means they can be found elsewhere in this book. Use the Index to find them.

Please note: We've avoided curse words, vulgar sexual words, and vulgar references to drugs in this book. For information on these types of terms, we recommend the *Oxford Dictionary of Slang* (John Ayato and John Simpson, editors).

1

Life on Campus—From Academics to Dormitory Life

In this chapter, we cover everything from academic slang to dorm slang . . . in short, everything we could think of that relates to life on a college campus.

101 (adj) ○ At most colleges, classes are coded by number to indicate difficulty, with **101** being the most basic level. **101** has been adopted into common speech to indicate something that is basic or easy.

*You didn't open the car door for Maria? Come on, man, that's dating **101**.*

ace (v) ○ To **ace** an exam is to get a grade of A. When people are sure that they've done well on an exam, they say they **aced** it.

Woman 1: I think I <u>flunked</u> my literature midterm.

*Woman 2: You should have <u>hit the books</u> like I did—I definitely **aced** that exam.*

bird classes (n) ○ These are classes that are so easy that you fly through them like a bird.

*My classes are so hard this semester, except for bowling—what a **bird class** that is.*

bloody paper (n) ○ Professors often grade students' work with red pen, and a paper that is returned to the student all marked up with red pen is called a **bloody paper**, because there are so many corrections written in red that the page looks like it's bleeding.

*I thought I did such a good job on my term paper, but when I got it back from the professor, it was completely **bloody**!*

blue book (n) ○ This is a small book with a blue cover filled with lined paper. Many professors require blue books for essay exams; some will provide them to you, but at some schools, you are required to purchase a blue book yourself (they cost approximately 15 cents each) and bring it to the exam.

*Man 1: Professor Jones, I forgot my **blue book**.*

*Man 2: Lucky for you, I have an extra **blue book**; otherwise, you would have to run to the bookstore to get one, and that would not leave you much time to complete the exam.*

bone up (v) ○ To **bone up** is to study all of the facts you need to know for an exam.

*I'm feeling pretty good about my math test tomorrow, but I need to **bone up** on my geometry, because I don't understand it as well as the algebra and I really want to ace the test.*

brownie points (n) ◯ If you do something that puts you in good favor with your professor, whether you have done extra credit work or just made an effort to participate in class and be noticed, you earn **brownie points.** This expression is derived from the Girl Scouts of America, whose junior members are called brownies and who earn points for completing a variety of tasks. Earning **brownie points** is a good idea, but do not go so overboard that you become a <u>brownnoser.</u>

*I stopped by Professor Chadwick's office yesterday, and she was swamped grading English <u>101</u> papers, so I helped her out and earned some major **brownie points.***

brownnoser (adj) ◯ **Brownnosers** are sycophants—people who go out of their way to flatter and ingratiate themselves with a professor with the distinct purpose of getting better grades. Please note: Being a **brownnoser** goes way beyond taking the time to get to know a professor—you should always get to know your professors; just don't be annoying about it.

*Ugh! Diana is such a **brownnoser**! Not only does she deliver coffee to Professor Cluck every morning, but she also shines his shoes!*

buckle down (v) ◯ To **buckle down** is to commit yourself to studying in a serious way without distractions.

*I've been doing nothing but partying since the semester began. I really need to **buckle down** if I don't want to <u>flunk</u> all of my classes this semester.*

bunk beds (n) ◯ These are two beds stacked on top of one another to save space. <u>Dorm</u> rooms are notoriously small, so many have **bunk beds.**

*Do you mind if I take the top **bunk bed**?*

buyback (n) ○ Where do all of those used books in the bookstore come from? They come from other students, of course! At the end of every semester (or year, depending on the school), colleges will buy back your books. Sounds great, right? Well, don't get too excited. The school pays a highly discounted price for the books, say, $5 for a $75 book, and many of the books you purchased will be ineligible for **buyback** for a number of reasons. Look for local bookstores that buy books back from students because they often buy them back at a higher rate than the school's official bookstore.

*This semester I paid $450 for my books. I went to the **buyback**, and I was able to sell five of my books back—for a total of $20!*

catch up (v) ○ When you miss a class, you need to **catch up**—do the work you've missed so you will be on the same level as your classmates who have not missed any classes. If you miss a lot of classes, you may find yourself playing **catch up.**

*Woman 1: Miss Thomas, you have missed three classes in a row! You are far behind the rest of the class. How do you plan to **catch up**?*

Woman 2: I will study an extra 3 hours a day and do any additional reading that you can recommend.

caught red-handed (v) ○ People who are cheating can be caught after the fact, or they can be **caught red-handed**, which means caught at the moment they were actually cheating. People can be **caught red-handed** doing other things, even serious things such as robbery.

*Jolie is going to be expelled for cheating—she was **caught red-handed**, reading the answers off her shoe!*

clue (someone) in (v) ❍ To **clue someone in** is to let that person know what is going on or to explain something to someone. If you miss a class, for example, you may need a classmate to **clue you in** about anything you missed in class.

> Man: *I didn't understand the professor today when she was talking about feminist theory in the twentieth century.*

> Woman: *Why don't we go get a cup of coffee and I can* **clue you in***?*

couch potato (n) ❍ This term denotes someone who possesses a high degree of laziness. So, if your roommate does nothing but sit around on the couch (or bed) all day and watch television, she's a **couch potato.**

> *Man, you're such a* **couch potato***! Why don't you come out and play volleyball with us instead of playing video games! Are you surgically attached to the couch?*

crack the books (v) ❍ To **crack the books** is to study hard. A synonym is **hit the books.**

> *I really need to* **crack the books** *if I'm going to do well on my midterm exam.*

cram (v) ○ This word is used frequently on campus. To **cram** is to study as much information as possible at the <u>last minute</u> and refers to literally stuffing your brain with information. This is not a good way to study. It's much better to study a little bit every night than to try to learn an entire semester's worth of work in one night.

*I haven't done any of the reading for anthropology this semester, and I <u>cut class</u> tons of times, and now I have to **cram** for the final tomorrow! I have one night to read 500 pages of text and to go over class notes that I borrowed from a friend.*

crash pad (n) ○ The place where someone sleeps is his or her **crash** (sleep) **pad** (dwelling). This is often shortened to **pad.**

*Want to come back to my **pad** to study? My <u>roommate</u> is out of town, so it's quiet there.*

cream of the crop (adj) ○ This term describes the best of something; for instance, the best students or the best athletes would be the **cream of the crop.**

*Law schools are looking to admit only the **cream of the crop,** so I need to get excellent grades to get into law school.*

cut class (v) ⊃ To **cut class** is to intentionally not attend a class for the purpose of doing something else. The "something else" can range from social plans to sleeping. Cutting class is not advised. It's hard to learn if you are not in class, and, hey, you *paid* for the class, so you might as well attend and get your money's worth. Some professors also have attendance policies, such as if you miss more than a certain number of classes, you fail. A synonym is **skip class**.

*I **cut** my 8 a.m. **class** two times last week because I was too tired to go, and I missed a pop quiz! The professor gave me a <u>zero</u> and said that if I miss one more class, he's going to <u>flunk</u> me!*

deadline (n) ⊃ A **deadline** is the date that a paper or a project is due to be handed in to a professor.

*I have so many **deadlines** to keep track of! I wish professors would get together and decide on one due date for all schoolwork.*

dorm (n) ⊃ **Dorm** is an abbreviated slang term for dormitory, which is the place on campus where students are housed. Your room is your **dorm room.** You will hear the term **dorm** all the time; you probably won't hear anyone use "dormitory."

*I hate living in the **dorm**. I can't wait to move <u>off campus</u> next year.*

drained (adj) ⊃ To be extremely tired or devoid of any ability to study or do anything is to be **drained.** Hard work **drains** your energy; for instance, you may be **drained** if you spend all night <u>cramming</u> for an exam.

*I have classes every day, as well as track practice and my volunteer work. By the time the weekend comes, I'm so **drained** that I can't even go out and party.*

drop a class (v) ◯ When you decide to remove yourself from a class, it's called **dropping a class.** You must **drop classes** at the beginning of the semester to avoid having the drop show up on your transcripts. You should only drop a class if you can't handle the coursework or have other extenuating circumstances.

*My parents are going to kill me! I have to **drop** Chemistry <u>101</u>; I don't understand anything, and I can't afford to have a failing grade on my transcript.*

dry campus (n) ◯ If your campus is a **dry campus**, it means that alcohol is illegal to possess or drink anywhere on campus. You might also hear **dry** used to describe other things as alcohol-free, such as fraternities or <u>dorms</u>.

*There are no bars on campus here, because it's a **dry campus.** We have to go to another town to get a beer!*

easy A's (adj) ◯ **Easy A's** are classes that are so easy that you can easily earn an A.

*I'm taking fishing and bowling this semester—I need a couple of **easy A's** to balance out my schedule. The rest of my classes are impossibly hard!*

fire drill (n) ◯ A **fire drill** is when the fire alarms go off in the <u>dorm</u> for the purpose of making every resident practice evacuating the building. On most campuses, you can get in big trouble if you stay in your room during a fire drill, which you should never do—there could be a real fire! **Fire drills** often happen at inconvenient times during the evening.

*We had a **fire drill** at 10 p.m. last night! Jennifer slept through it and was fined $100!*

flip-flops (n) ○ Also called *thongs,* **flip-flops** are rubber sandals held on the feet by two straps that meet between the first and second toes; so named because of the "flip-flop" sound they make when someone is walking. This has become a fashionable and common kind of shoe on college campuses this past year. It is a good idea to get yourself a pair of cheap **flip-flops** to wear in the shower in your <u>dorm</u> to avoid foot fungus. Really! (We could have included this definition in Chapter 7, but **flip-flops** are an integral part of dorm life.)

*I couldn't find my **flip-flops** this morning, so I showered without them, and now my feet itch!*

flunk (v) ○ To **flunk** is to fail a class. If you fail too many classes, you can **flunk** out of school.

*I am going to **flunk** out of school if I don't <u>buckle</u> <u>down</u>.*

freshman 15 (n) ○ It is said that everyone gains 15 pounds during their freshman year—blame the dining hall and late-night pizzas—called the **freshman 15.** Some people don't gain any weight freshman year, and some gain more than 15 pounds. Please note: Underage drinking is illegal in the United States, but many freshmen gain much of their weight from beer, which is very fattening.

*I never thought I would gain the fabled **freshman 15** at college, and I didn't. I gained 30 pounds!*

frosh (n) ○ A **frosh** is a member of the freshman class. **Frosh** can also be used to describe someone who is new to something.

> *Woman 1: Doesn't that annoying girl know not to ask questions at the*
> *end of class?*
>
> *Woman 2: She's a silly **frosh**, not a wise sophomore like you. She*
> *doesn't know any better.*

futon (n) ○ Of Japanese origin, a **futon** is a bed with a flat, usually wooden, base with a soft mattress that converts into a couch when not being used as a bed. You will find many futons on a college campus.

> *I bought a used **futon** from a graduating senior for $50! It will be*
> *perfect for my apartment.*

get away with (v) ○ To **get away with** something is to do something bad or incorrect without suffering any consequences. We've included this with the academic terms because students are always trying to **get away with** stuff when it comes to class.

> *Man 1: You better start coming to class. You can't get away with <u>cutting</u>*
> *all semester!*
>
> *Man 2: I can **get away with** anything. My father donates millions of*
> *dollars a year to the school, so they have to pass me!*

get the hang of something (v) ○ When someone becomes familiar with a task or routine, they **get the hang of it.** We've included this term here because you may often hear it used in an academic situation.

> *I can't seem to **get the hang of** how to study in college. It seemed so*
> *much easier in high school, but I guess I'll learn.*

hard core (adj) ↻ When applied to studying, **hard core** means to focus on nothing else but studying.

> *Man 1: Are you going to the football game this Saturday?*
>
> *Man 2: No. I've got a huge exam to study for, so I'm going **hard core**. I won't think about anything else but history for the next three days!*

hit the books (v) ↻ See **crack the books.**

hit the rack (v) ↻ To **hit the rack** is to go to sleep, the rack being the bed.

> *I've been up since 6 a.m.! I can't wait to **hit the rack**!*

homecoming (n) ↻ **Homecoming** is an event weekend in college when alumni come back to visit, and there is usually a football game. In other words, the alumni are coming "home" to the school. At some schools, **homecoming** weekend is a huge event, and students party all weekend. At other schools, it is not such a big deal.

> *This weekend is **homecoming** weekend! All of my friends who graduated last year are coming back, and we're going to have a huge party after the football game.*

homecoming king/queen (n) ↻ At <u>homecoming</u>, there is often a ceremony where a **homecoming king** and a **homecoming queen** are crowned. Not every school has this tradition, and of those that do, the qualifications necessary to be crowned vary greatly.

> *I can't wait to be crowned **homecoming queen**. It's nice to be recognized for my community service.*

Jaffa blocks (n) ◌ These are plastic crates that can be stacked one on top of the other. They can be used to store everything from clothing to books. You'll see a lot of these—as well as milk crates—used as <u>dorm</u> room furniture.

I don't know what I'd do without my **Jaffa blocks!** *I could never fit all of my clothes into my tiny* <u>dorm</u> *room closet!*

jump to conclusions (v) ◌ When people make assumptions about something or someone without considering all the facts, they **jump to conclusions.** This is something you might hear professors say quite often, as in "don't **jump to conclusions** without doing all of the reading first."

*I thought that Professor Dune's class would be easy because he's a new professor, but I really **jumped to conclusions.** He's new to this school, but he's been teaching for thirty years and his class is really difficult!*

john (n) ◌ **John** is slang for "bathroom." If someone asks where the **john** is, show him or her to the bathroom.

*I really have to use the **john**! I drank a jumbo coffee this morning, and I've been sitting in class all day with no break.*

lab (n) ◌ A **lab** is an auxiliary class to a main class, usually a science class, in which students perform hands-on tasks to learn material. For instance, in a chemistry class, you would learn about how chemical reactions work, but in your chemistry **lab**, you would actually mix chemicals to produce reactions.

*I have biology every day! Monday, Wednesday, and Thursday I have class, and I have **lab** on Tuesday and Thursday.*

last minute (adv) ◯ This expression means "the latest possible time." Many students, for example, wait until the day before a paper is due (or the night before) to write it; this is the **last minute.**

> Man: *I can't believe the book I need for my 20-page paper has been checked out of the library! The paper is due tomorrow!*
>
> Woman: *Well, you shouldn't have waited until the **last minute** to write your paper. I finished mine three days ago.*

loft (n) ◯ A **loft** is a raised platform in a room with a bed on it, often built in dorm rooms to save space. Please note: Most universities don't provide lofts; instead, students build them. Lofts are not allowed in all dorms, so be careful before you get one—it may not be structurally sound.

*I bought a **loft** from two graduating seniors, so now my bed is raised off the floor and my roommate and I have twice as much space.*

lounge (n) ◯ Some dorms have common areas on each floor with couches and a television that are called **lounges.**

*I hate hanging out in the **lounge**. No one can ever agree on which TV show to watch.*

mall (n) ◯ Some campuses refer to the central area of campus as the **mall,** some schools refer to this area as a **quad,** and some schools have no name for the main area. **Mall** also means a place where there is a group of retail stores for shopping, so many students (including students native to the United States) are confused when they hear **mall** used to describe a central area of campus. (Also see page 76)

*My history professor held class outside in the **mall** today. It was really nice to sit outside, but all of the students walking from class to class were distracting.*

mini-fridge (n) ○ A **mini-fridge** is a very small refrigerator. Many colleges offer students the opportunity to rent **mini-fridges** to keep in their rooms. Some schools offer **mini-fridge/microwave** combinations.

*I rented a **mini-fridge** for my room, and it's so small that my <u>roommate</u> and I can barely fit all of our stuff in it.*

multiple guess (adj) ○ A **multiple-guess** test is a multiple-choice test taken by someone who does not know any of the answers, so that person makes multiple guesses.

Man 1: I thought that math test was so easy! I love multiple choice.

*Man 2: **Multiple guess** is more like it for me! I didn't know even one answer!*

nuke (v) ○ To **nuke** something is to cook it in the microwave.

*I **nuked** some popcorn, and I left it in so long that it got burned!*

off campus (n) ○ This term describes anything that is not within the bounds of campus or is not controlled by the school. This term is mostly used in conjunction with jobs or housing.

*I found a great apartment **off campus**, and it's cheaper than the <u>dorms</u>!*

office hours (n) ○ In addition to teaching classes, all professors do office work. You may see professors in their offices during certain times of the week, which are called **office hours.** You should know when each of your professors has **office hours**, in case you need to speak to your professor about something.

> Woman 1: *Aren't you coming back to the* <u>dorm</u>? *It's almost dinnertime.*
>
> Woman 2: *I'll be a little late for dinner tonight. I'm going to see Professor Davis in her office. It's too bad her* **office hours** *aren't during lunchtime, because I'm starving!*

on the curve (adv) ○ Some professors grade tests and papers **on the curve.** The most common way of grading **on the curve** is when scores are adjusted after the exam is scored based on the highest score. So, if the highest score any student got was a 90, that score becomes 100 and every lower score is raised by 10 points.

> *I'm so* <u>psyched</u>! *I thought I failed my exam, but the professor grades* **on the curve**, *so I actually ended up with a passing score!*

Parents' weekend (n) ○ **Parents' weekend** is a weekend during the school year when parents, family, and friends can visit students and get a feel for campus life.

> *It's* **parents' weekend** *and all of the restaraunts on campus are booked, so my parents and I stayed in my room and ordered a pizza.*

play hooky (v) ○ To **play hooky** is to <u>cut class</u>, but **playing hooky** usually implies intentionally missing a whole day of class instead of just one class.

> *There's this concert I just have to go to, so I'm* **playing hooky** *tomorrow to go see it. It's totally worth missing three classes!*

plow through (v) ⊙ When someone **plows through** something, he or she works on it with great determination.

*I have to read 150 pages of history text in two days and create an outline—I'm going to just have to **plow through** it to get it done.*

pop quiz (n) ⊙ A **pop quiz** is a surprise quiz. This is something you will run into quite often in college. Some professors like to use **pop quizzes** to make sure everyone is paying attention and attending class.

*I have Spanish five times a week, and I never go to every class, but yesterday, I missed a **pop quiz**, and the professor gave me a <u>zero</u>. I can't miss anymore classes, because if I miss one more **pop quiz**, I'll <u>flunk</u>.*

prof (n) ⊙ **Prof** is an abbreviation of "professor."

    *Man: Who's your psych **prof**?*

Woman: Professor McKinley.

pull an all-nighter (v) ⊙ When a person stays awake all night to study or finish a paper or project, he or she **pulls an all-nighter.** You will hear this expression quite often, because college students are notorious for delaying study until the <u>last minute</u>, causing them to have to stay up all night. This is a bad study habit. You will often be so tired on the morning of your exam that you will be unable to function normally.

Woman 1: Wow, you look really tired!

*Woman 2: I haven't slept all night! I had to **pull an all-nighter** to study for my chemistry exam. I wish I had started studying earlier—I almost fell asleep while I was taking the test!*

RA (n) ○ **RA** is an abbreviation of Resident Assistant. **RAs** are students who, in exchange for free room and board (or other perks, depending on the school), live in the <u>dorms</u> and act as advisers for the students in the dormitories. They are often also charged with making sure all residents adhere to the rules, and they act as mediators and counselors for students who need help.

*My **RA** really helped my <u>roommate</u> and me resolve our problems living together.*

rents (n) ○ **Rents** is an abbreviation of pa**rents.** You will commonly hear people refer to their **rents.**

*This apartment is a mess and my **rents** are going to be here soon! My mom will be horrified at this mess!*

rain closet (n) ○ **Rain closet** is slang for "shower."

*I always wear my <u>flip-flops</u> in the **rain closet.***

ripped it apart (v) ○ When an assignment is handed back to you with a bad grade and many criticisms, it has been **ripped apart** by your professor.

*I got a D on my creative writing assignment. My <u>prof</u> hated it! She really **ripped it apart;** it's literally covered in red pen!*

rock an exam (v) ○ To **rock an exam** is to do very well. This term is synonymous with <u>ace</u>, but is a more modern term.

*I really **rocked that exam!** I'll get into a top grad school for sure now!*

rocks for jocks (n) ○ Rocks for jocks refers to a low-level geology class, such as Geology <u>101</u>, but can be used to describe any <u>bird</u> <u>class</u>. This term plays on the stereotype that athletes, or <u>jocks</u>, are not smart, so they take easy classes to get good grades and be eligible for their sports. This is not a phrase you should use, because it's not very nice, but you may hear it on campus.

> Woman: *Why are you taking beginner's geology? You don't like science.*
>
> Man: *It's **rocks for jocks**. It will be easy to pass!*

roommate (n) ○ Your **roommate** is the person with whom you share your room or living quarters. Some people get along really well with their roommates, whereas others don't; if you have a serious problem with your roommate, see your <u>RA</u>.

> *My **roommate** and I are total opposites, so we had to get used to living together.*

shape up (v) ○ If your professor tells you to **shape up,** it means you must work harder and do a better job in class than you have been doing. **Shape up** can also be a command meaning *behave.*

> *Mr. Wilson, you better **shape up** if you expect to pass my class. I will not tolerate <u>slackers</u>!*

sink or swim (v) ○ **Sink or swim** means either to not do well (**sink**) or to do well (**swim**), with the implication that if you don't do well, the consequences will be dire. College is basically a **sink-or-swim** situation; if you **sink,** you can lose the opportunity to complete your education.

> *The auditions for the campus musical productions are **sink or swim**; you only get one chance to do well and impress the director.*

stick your neck out (v) ○ To **stick your neck out** is to take a big chance to help out someone, which could result in a bad ending for you. In other words, you are helping out someone else possibly at your own expense.

Woman 1: I really need help writing my paper. It's due tomorrow!

*Woman 2: If I **stick my neck out** for you, I might not be able to finish my own paper, so you're on you own. Sorry.*

study buddy (n) ○ A **study buddy** is a study partner. It is a good idea to make a friend in class to study with or to join a study group, which is a group of people in the same class who get together and study.

*Thank goodness for Alicia; she's the best **study buddy** I've ever had! Ever since we started studying together, I haven't gotten below a B on a quiz!*

super senior (n) ○ American colleges used to have an average graduation rate of four years, but recently, many students began taking more time to graduate for a variety of reasons. Students who are past their fourth year of college and have not yet graduated are often called **super seniors.**

*Angie's <u>boyfriend</u> has been going to this school for seven years, so he's like a **super super super senior**.*

syllabus (n) ○ This term is not really slang or an idiom, but it is specific to college, so we've included it here. On the first day of class, many professors provide students with a schedule that outlines what each class will cover and includes dates of exams and other important dates. Don't lose it; and if you do, get another one quickly!

*My **syllabus** for economics is scary! There are four exams, and there's a quiz every other class!*

take notes (v) ○ To **take notes** is to make notations in a notebook about what you are learning while in class. Many professors give tests that center on class discussions and not just about readings, so your class notes are very important. If you miss a class, ask a friend if you can copy his or her notes.

My world civilization class is packed with information. I take notes from the very second class begins until we're dismissed. I'm on my second notebook already!

TA (n) ○ **TA** is short for Teaching Assistant. Many colleges have classes that are taught by **TAs,** who are usually graduate students who assist the teachers. At other schools, **TAs** are simply present in your class to assist the professor and to help the students. If you have a problem or a question and are intimidated by the professor, ask the **TA,** who often seems more approachable. It's the TA's job to help you.

The TA in my art history class is so nice. She sat with me for half an hour after class last week and explained the building of the pyramids in Egypt.

teacher's pet (n) ○ A **teacher's pet** is a <u>brownnoser</u> whom the teacher seems to favor.

I hate Amy. She brings the professor cookies once a week, and he thinks she's the best! She's such a teacher's pet.

term paper (n) ○ A **term paper** is a large research paper, usually one that takes the entire semester (or *term*) to complete.

I haven't done a bit of work on my term paper, and now I have only three weeks to finish it!

up to speed (adj) ○ When someone misses a class, he or she must find out what was missed to catch up, or to be **up to speed.**

*You had better study and get **up to speed** with all the classes you missed, or you're going to <u>flunk</u> out of school!*

upperclassman (n) ○ Upperclassmen are all students who are juniors and seniors (and <u>super</u> <u>seniors</u>!). Freshmen and sophomores are **underclassmen.**

*I'm taking an advanced financial theory class, and I'm the only freshman! The rest of the class are **upperclassmen** and graduate students!*

zero (n) ○ A student who does not study, pay attention, and attend classes will most likely receive a **zero**, or a failing grade, for the class or a particular exam.

*I know I wasn't prepared for the test, so I shouldn't be surprised that I got a **zero** on the midterm.*

2

Be Social—Conversation and Communication

All words in the English language (or any other language) are used for conversation and communication. (Technically, all the words in this book can be considered part of the category of conversation or communication.) For this chapter, we've chosen words common to all sorts of conversations, including greetings, words asking for information, words about friendship, and words about arguments.

4-1-1 (n) ◌ **4-1-1** means "information." So, if someone asks you, "What's the **4-1-1**?" he or she is asking, "What is the information?" This term originated from the fact that in many parts of the United States, you can dial the numbers 4-1-1 on your telephone to be connected with an "information" operator to obtain a local telephone number.

*Woman 1: What's the **4-1-1** on Becky and Max?*
Woman 2: They had a huge fight last night.

a fly on the wall (n) ↻ This is part of the larger expression of "I'd like to be a **fly on the wall** during that conversation," which means "I'd really like to have heard what those people were saying."

Man 1: Joey's <u>girlfriend</u> found out he was <u>cheating</u> on her.

*Man 2: Wow, I'd love to be a **fly on the wall** when she confronts him!*

add fuel to the fire (v) ↻ When you provide information that makes a person more angry about something than he or she had previously been angry about, you **add fuel to the fire.**

*Don't **add fuel to the fire** by telling your <u>roommate</u> that your other roommate said she was a <u>loser</u>.*

ad-lib (v) ↻ To **ad-lib** is to improvise or to make up something as you are doing it.

*I totally forgot I had to give a presentation in class today, so I **ad-libbed,** and I think the professor actually thought I knew what I was talking about.*

all right (adv) ↻ **All right** is an affirmative answer to a question. It is used the same way as "okay."

***All right,** I'll do it.*

Audi 500 (adv) ↻ This expression derived from the expression "I'm outtie," which means "I'm leaving." (*Outtie* sounds like the name of the car, **Audi**.)

*I'm **Audi 500.** It's way past my bedtime.*

back off (v) ☉ When someone tells you to **back off,** he or she means "leave me alone," or "mind your own business."

*Why don't you just **back off**! I don't want to fight with you!*

bad-mouth (v) ☉ To **bad-mouth** someone is to speak poorly of that person, often to common friends.

*She totally **bad-mouthed** me to this guy I like, and now he won't even say hello to me!*

bail (v) ☉ To **bail** is to leave. Some synonyms are **bounce, jet,** and **out like trout.**

*I've got to **bail**. Hope you enjoy the rest of your night.*

beat around the bush (v) ☉ If you are afraid to tell someone else something, you may **beat around the bush** by telling that person everything *but* the important thing.

*Don't **beat around the bush**. Just tell me the truth!*

behind someone's back (adv) ☉ When you speak about someone **behind his or her back,** it means you say bad things about that person to other people but do not say bad things directly to the person about whom you are talking.

*My roommate pretended to be my friend; meanwhile, she was **talking behind my back** to my other friends and saying really bad things about me!*

big mouth (n) ❍ Someone who is a **big mouth** talks too much and usually tells people things that shouldn't be said.

*My friend is such a **big mouth**! I told her a secret, and she told everyone on my floor!*

blower (n) ❍ A **blower** is a telephone. This is a fairly new slang phrase.

*Get off the **blower**, I have to make a call.*

bone to pick (adj) ❍ If you have a **bone to pick** with someone, it means you have a problem with that person or you are angry with that person.

*I have a **bone to pick** with you. Stop borrowing my clothes!*

bump into (v) ❍ When you see someone unexpectedly somewhere, you **bump into** him or her.

*I **bumped into** my freshman-year <u>roommate</u> on the <u>mall</u> today. I haven't seen him in two years!*

butt in (v) ❍ To **butt in** means to interrupt.

*Don't **butt in** on their conversation.*

check it out (v) ❍ Often used as a sentence opener, **check it out** means "investigate it" or "listen to this."

Check it out, *I got an A on my term paper!*

clear the air (v) ⊃ When people make amends after a disagreement, they **clear the air.**

*Can you and Kate please **clear the air**? You've been fighting for way too long.*

dillio (n) ⊃ This expression derived from the slang expression "what's the deal, yo," which means "what is going on?" Over time, the words *deal* and *yo* became combined into **dillio.**

*What's the **dillio**? Are we going to that party or not?*

dis (v) ⊃ **Dis** is a slang abbreviation of "**dis**respect." To **dis** someone is to treat that person poorly.

*Dave totally **dissed** me last night. We were supposed to hang out, and he went to a bar with his friends instead.*

fall out (v) ⊃ To **fall out** with someone is to have a disagreement with and to stop speaking to that person. If you are having a **falling out,** you are in the middle of a disagreement.

*My professor and I had a **falling out,** and I hope he still grades me well on my test in spite of it.*

fill me in (v) ⊃ When someone asks you to **"fill me in,"** he or she wants you to supply information on something.

*Can you please **fill me in** on what was discussed in class on Friday? I missed class because I was sick.*

gab (v) ◯ To **gab** is to speak. This often implies an extended conversation involving gossip.

*She and I **gabbed** for hours about our high school days.*

get the picture (v) ◯ To **get the picture** is to understand something.

*It's important that you don't tell him what I said, because it will make him very angry. **Get the picture?***

give it a rest (v) ◯ To **give it a rest** is to stop talking about something you have been talking about for some time or to stop focusing on an ongoing problem.

*Would you **give it a rest** already? I still do not want to go on a date with you!*

give me a hand (v) ◯ If someone asks you to "**give me a hand**," that person is asking you to help him or her out.

*Can you **give me a hand** with these boxes? They're too heavy for me to lift by myself.*

have a say (v) ◯ To **have a say** in something is to have influence and power to help make a decision on that thing.

*All students **have a say** in how well they do in this class. All they need to do is work hard.*

hey (n) ◯ This interjection means the same thing as *hello* or *hi*. There are many words for introductory greetings in the United States, but **hey** is one of the most popular.

***Hey**, how are you?*

high-five (n) ☉ A **high-five** is when two people slap each other's palm high in the air as a sign of triumph or celebration. The **five** refers to the five fingers on a hand.

*The basketball players were so happy to win the playoff game that they were giving each other **high-fives** all night.*

hit me up on my cell (v) ☉ This is a fairly recent phrase. **Hit me up** means "call me." This expression is commonly used to refer to cell phones but can also be used with landline phones and e-mail.

> Man: *Do you want to see a movie tonight?*
>
> Woman: *Sure, but I don't know what time I will be free. **Hit me up on my cell** in an hour, and I'll let you know.*

holla (n) ☉ This expression means "what's up?" or "hello."

> Man 1: <u>*Hey.*</u>
>
> Man 2: **Holla.**

how come? (n) ☉ This expression means "why" and is pervasive throughout the English language, mostly among younger people, used in place of "why."

> Man: *I can't go to the football game tonight.*
>
> Woman: **How come?**
>
> Man: *Because I have to study for a test.*

I got skills (v) ☉ When someone says "**I got skills,**" it means "I'm good at something" or "I'm good at everything." Often, the word *mad* is inserted before *skills:* **mad skills.**

*I **got skills** on the baseball field, but I **got mad skills** on the basketball court.*

I hear ya (v) ○ This means "I understand what you are saying." This is often used in conversation to let the speaker know that the listener is following along with the story. It is also often used as an expression of sympathy, sometimes worded "I hear that."

Woman 1: This class is too hard. I think I might flunk.

Woman 2: **I hear ya.** *I may fail as well.*

later (adv) ○ This is another quite common way to say good-bye.

Man 1: Good-bye. I'll see you tomorrow.

Man 2: **Later.**

like (n) ○ Used as a meaningless sentence interjection while speaking, **like** is probably the most commonly used word among young people. It **like,** appears in **like,** many conversations that kids **like,** have. You may find yourself thrown off by this at first, but you'll get used to hearing it and you'll be able to discern the **likes** used as meaningless interjections and the **likes** used properly, that is, "I **like** math."

Do you think she **like,** *knows that her boyfriend is* **like,** *also seeing another girl?*

make waves (v) ○ To **make waves** is to cause problems or disruptions.

My professor doesn't like students who **make waves** *in class by disagreeing with what he says.*

my bad (n) ◯ **My bad** means "I'm sorry," or "I've made a mistake or done something bad."

> Woman: *You spilled your soup all over me!*
>
> Man: *Oh!* **My bad.** *Let me buy you another cup of soup and pay for your cleaning to make it up to you.*

no way (n) ◯ **No way** means NO! It can also indicate something that is impossible.

> *There is* **no way** *she is going to pass the driving test. She doesn't have her glasses on!*

nunya (n) ◯ **Nunya** means "none of your business" or "it does not concern you." This slang term is derived from the blending together of *none* and *your* from the phrase "none of your business."

> Woman 1: *What were you guys talking about?*
>
> Woman 2: **Nunya.** *So, please leave us alone.*

out (v, n) ◯ **Out** has several meanings. (1) To be **out** on something is to not want to do something. (2) **Out** is also used in place of good-bye; derived from "I'm out of here." You may sometimes hear it used in a larger, silly expression, like **out like trout** or **peace out.** (Also see page 105)

> *I'm* **out** *on bungee jumping. It's too dangerous.*

paint a picture (v) ◯ If someone asks you to **paint a picture** of something in the course of conversation, that person is asking you to supply him or her with a detailed description of something.

> *Can you* **paint me a picture** *so I can understand better the look you want?*

peeps (n) ◯ Your **peeps** are your friends. **Peeps** is short for "people."

*My **peeps** and I are having a huge party tonight.*

play devil's advocate (v) ◯ To **play devil's advocate** is to present a view on something for the sake of argument, not necessarily because you agree with the view.

*Okay, class, we've spoken about one way to build a bridge using machines, but let me **play devil's advocate** here and suggest that we think of a way to build a bridge should machines not be available.*

put your foot in your mouth (v) ◯ When you say something to someone that is unintentionally rude or insulting, you have **put your foot in your mouth.**

Woman 1: I was talking about how I thought blondes were not smart in front of Linda, who's blonde! I felt so bad.

*Woman 2: Wow! You really **put your foot in your mouth.***

short for (adv) ◯ **Short for** means "an abbreviation."

*Mandie is **short for** the name Amanda.*

shut up (v) ◯ To **shut up** means "to be quiet." This is a harsh and an impolite thing to say to someone.

***Shut up!** I don't want to hear you talk anymore.*

simmer down now (v) ◯ This means "relax." Some synonyms are **take it easy** and **chill out.**

*Just **simmer down now**. There is no reason to panic.*

small talk (n) ○ Sometimes called **chit-chat, small talk** is superficial conversation. You may make **small talk** with someone you don't know very well.

*That's enough with the **small talk**. Let's talk about something serious.*

sounds good (v) ○ **Sounds good** means "that is a good idea."

Woman: *Why don't we go to the movies tonight?*

Man: ***Sounds good.** I'll pick you up at 8:00.*

speak up (v) ○ This is a command telling someone to voice his or her opinion.

*If you don't **speak up** in class, you're going to get a poor grade, because class participation is a part of the final grade.*

'sup (v) ○ This is a slang abbreviation of "what's up," meaning, "how are you?" or "what is going on?" A synonym is **wazzup.**

Man 1: ***'Sup?***

Man 2: *Nothing. How are you?*

take sides (v) ○ There are two sides to every argument, and if you feel strongly about one side of the argument and act on that feeling, you have **taken sides.**

*I don't want to **take sides** in this argument! The two of you will just have to work it out yourselves!*

tell someone off (v) ○ To **tell someone off** is to say mean things out of anger to someone who has wronged you.

*That boy said I was ugly, so I **told him off** in class and then got in trouble for using curse words!*

two cents' worth (n) ○ Your **two cents' worth** is your advice to someone.

*If you want my **two cents' worth,** I think you should be a psych major.*

wax poetic (v) ○ To **wax poetic** is to speak at length about a single subject.

*My professor loves to **wax poetic** about Civil War-era fashion. He spent the whole class yesterday lecturing on the clothing of soldiers!*

what about . . .? (v) ○ This phrase is spoken before making a suggestion. It means "why don't we do . . ." or "I have a suggestion." The verb is usually left out of the suggestion that follows; for example, "**What about** bowling?" means "Why don't we go bowling?"

Man 1: What do you want to do tonight?

*Man 2: **What about** the party down the block?*

Man 1: Sounds good.

what's up? ○ (v) **What's up?** is another way to say "hello" or "how are you?"

Woman 1: Hi, Alysha?

Woman 2: What's up, Megan?

word (v) ◯ **Word** means "that's <u>cool</u>" or "I agree."

> Man: *This is my favorite band.*

> Woman: **Word.** *I love them, too.*

yo (n) ◯ **Yo** is one of the most common slang terms you'll encounter. It is an expression used to get someone's attention or as an informal form of address. It can also mean hello. It is usually used at the beginning of a sentence (**Yo,** what's up?) or at the end of a sentence (What's up, **yo?**).

Yo! Over there! Can you hear me?

3

Let's Party!—And Be Safe

A party is a festive gathering of people, and college is a great place to find lots of different kinds of parties. Given this fact, it's no surprise that there are probably thousands of words you'll hear in college that relate to partying in some way. We couldn't possibly list them all here—it would take years. But in this chapter, you'll find a good sampling of words that you're likely to hear. The drinking of alcohol takes place at many college parties unless your school has a dry (alcohol-prohibited) campus. You may not hang out with people who drink for fun, but you'll still need to know the terminology, so you can at least make fun of those drunken people. We've also included some words about illegal substances, because we want you to know what to be careful of.

action (n) ◯ **Action** is a word for a party or a place where there is a good <u>scene</u>. This word is often used in a question, such as "Where's the **action**?" meaning, where is a good place to go or party to have fun for the night.

> *Man 1: Hey, is there any **action** tonight? I'd love to see what's happening downtown.*
>
> *Man 2: Nah. There's never any **action** in this town. There's nothing to do here!*

all banged up (v) ○ This is how you might feel after a night of partying . . . which is terrible. See *wasted* for an alternate definition.

> *I'm **all banged up** today, I stayed out way too late last night, and I feel like I could sleep for hours!*

antifreeze (n) ○ **Antifreeze** in this sense means alcohol and usually refers to very strong liquor that has a strong taste but it can also be used as a general term.

> *Ugh! This vodka is terrible! Who brought this **antifreeze**?*

bar crawl (n) ○ Many college towns and cities have areas that are filled with bars and thus, filled with people. When you begin the night at one bar and then move around to different bars throughout the night, you are on a **bar crawl.** Some places, such as downtown Philadelphia, have official bar crawls during holidays, such as Halloween, where the city provides safe bus transportation to bar patrons so they can visit all of the bars.

> *I'm graduating this week, and my friends and I are going on a total **bar crawl** tonight. We're going to have a drink and hang out at every bar that we've ever been in before in town.*

bash (n) ○ A **bash** is a large party. A synonym is **blowout.** This term has been around for a while, so you might even encounter school-sponsored functions with **bash** in the name, such as "The Spring **Bash**" or "The Halloween **Bash**."

> *Hey, the guys down the street are having a huge **bash** tonight with a band and lots of food. I can't wait to go!*

beer funnel (n) ○ A **beer funnel** is a large plastic funnel with a hose attached to the small end. A can of beer is poured down the funnel and through the hose into a person's mouth (sometimes called just a **funnel** or **funneling**). **Warning:** You will get very drunk from doing this and you just might <u>puke</u>—or you could end up in the hospital or die.

*Mario was doing a **beer funnel** at this huge party, and he <u>puked</u> right after he was done in front of <u>like</u>, 100 people!*

blotto (adj) ○ Someone who is **blotto** is extremely intoxicated and probably not in complete control of himself or herself. Some synonyms are **blasted, blitzed, bombed, lit, plastered, stoned,** and **zonked.**

*Sharon drank way too much <u>booze</u> tonight; she's so **blotto** that she probably won't remember anything that happened tonight when she wakes up in the morning.*

boogie (v) ○ To **boogie** means to dance, but it can also be used as a general term that means "to party." A synonym is **get down.**

*Amy's a great dancer. She goes to clubs to **boogie** all night.*

boot and rally (v) ○ This is a vulgar way to refer to the action of vomiting from drinking too much and then continuing to party and drink afterward. This is an ill-advised action.

Man 1: I'm so sick. I just <u>puked</u> everything I drank tonight.
*Man 2: Come on <u>dude</u>, **boot and rally**! It's too early to stop partying.*
Man 1: Are you crazy? I'm not that stupid. I'm going home to <u>sleep it off</u>.

booze (n) ◯ **Booze** is a generic term for alcohol. It is sometimes used as part of a verb phrase that means "to drink": **booze it up.**

*I hope there's no **booze** at this party tonight . . . drunk people really annoy me.*

booze cruise (n) ◯ A **booze cruise** is a boat with a bar on it that sails out on the ocean for a couple of hours with a group of partying people. **Booze cruises** are usually found in popular vacation spots near water, most notably, on tropical islands.

*We went on this awesome **booze cruise** in Cancun, but I didn't drink, so I actually got to enjoy being on the boat as opposed to all the drunk people who got sick.*

break it up (v) ◯ This is what you might hear if you're at a party and the police show up and make everyone go home—they say, "**Break it up.**" This also acts as a command to tell people to stop fighting.

*All right, folks, **break it up.** This party is too loud, and your neighbors complained; you all have to go home.*

brew (n) ◯ **Brew** is one of the countless words for beer. Some other words for beer are **swill, brewsky, brew-ha,** and **suds**.

*There's nothing like an ice-cold **brew** to <u>wash down</u> a juicy hamburger.*

butts (n) ◯ **Butts** is a slang term for cigarettes. It also refers to crushed, already-smoked cigarettes.

*Bonnie and I had a party at our apartment last night, and the place is such a mess now. There are **butts** all over the floor, and the apartment smells like an ashtray!*

buzzed (adj) ◯ This means to be a little bit drunk—usually said when someone finally begins to feel the effects of any substances he or she might have taken. Someone who is trying to become intoxicated is trying to **catch a buzz.**

*I've only had two beers, but I'm **buzzed**. It usually takes more beer for me to feel like this.*

BYOB, BYO (v) ◯ **BYOB** is an acronym for Bring Your Own Beer (or <u>Booze</u>), and is sometimes shortened to just **BYO** (Bring Your Own).

*Are you going to the big party tonight? It should be pretty fun, but it's **BYOB**, so we need to stop and get some beer if we want to drink.*

can't hold (your, his, her) drinks (v) ◯ People who get very drunk on a very small amount of alcohol or who can't handle being drunk **can't hold their drinks**. This does not mean that someone physically can't hold a drink in his or her hands (although if the person drinks enough, that just may be the case!).

*You're not drinking anything tonight, because you **can't hold your drinks** and I'm not carrying you home again!*

coke (n) ◯ This is a slang term for *cocaine*, which is an illegal and dangerous drug that is derived from the cocoa plant. It is an amphetamine, and a person can die and/or get in serious trouble with the law by using it or having it in his or her possession. Some synonyms are **charlie** and **C.**

*I wouldn't go out with Adam if I were you; he has a serious **coke** problem, and that's not good.*

crash (v) ◯ When you stay at someone else's house or <u>dorm</u> room after a night out, you **crash** (sleep) there.

*May I **crash** at your place after the movies tonight? It's going to be late, and I don't want to drive home then.*

designated driver (n) ◯ The **designated driver** is the person in a group of friends who does not drink any alcohol for the night, so that he or she can drive all of the friends safely home.

*Karen, thank you so much for being our **designated driver** tonight. It's so responsible of you!*

drinking problem (n) ◯ Someone who has a **drinking problem** drinks too much alcohol too often and may be addicted to alcohol. If someone does too many drugs, it is said that he or she has a **drug problem.** You may, however, hear this term used sarcastically—when someone accidentally spills a drink, they person may say he or she has a "drinking problem," which is taking the term quite literally.

*Jessie really has a **drinking problem.** I think she was drunk in class today—at 8 o'clock in the morning!*

E, X (n) ◯ Both **E** and **X** refer to "ecstasy," which is an illegal drug (MDMA) that can produce psychedelic effects and can be very dangerous. This is a drug that can kill you.

*This girl on my floor died last night after doing too much **X.***

feelin' no pain (v) ☺ Someone who is **feelin' no pain** is pleasantly drunk. This refers to the numbed senses that come from drinking.

> *Man 1: Corey's had too much to drink.*
>
> *Man 2: I know, he's **feelin' no pain,** but he will be in the morning when he wakes up with a <u>hangover</u>!*

GHB (n) ☺ **GHB** is a dangerous drug similar to anesthesia medicine that renders the person who ingests it so intoxicated and sedated that he or she often has no idea what he or she is doing and wakes up in the morning not knowing what happened the night before. It is also called the **date-rape** drug, because it is colorless and odorless, and when slipped into a person's drink, renders that person defenseless; people have deliberately done this to others with the intention of taking advantage of the victim sexually. **Warning:** Do not ever leave your drink (alcoholic or otherwise) unattended at a party; if you do, get a new one. We're not even going to give you a sample sentence for this one; we just want you to be careful.

gone on a bender (v) ☺ When someone goes for a long period of time drinking continuously, that person has **gone on a bender.**

> *Woman 1: Have you seen John lately?*
>
> *Woman 2: Yes, I saw him last night and he's **gone on a bender**. He's been drunk for three days! I really think he has a <u>drinking problem</u>.*

hair of the dog (n) ◯ The **hair of the dog** is alcohol drunk in the morning that is said to cure a <u>hangover</u>. There is no proof that this actually works, but a friend may advise you to do it at some point. Trust us—take an aspirin and drink lots of water instead.

> Man 1: *Why are you drinking vodka in the morning?*
>
> Man 2: *It's the **hair of the dog**, it's supposed to make you feel better.*
>
> Man 1: *Did it work?*
>
> Man 2: *No.*

hangover (n) ◯ That really terrible headache and dry mouth and sickness you wake up with after a night of drinking is a **hangover.** This term can also be used as a verb phrase: **hungover.**

> *Jennifer woke up with a terrible **hangover** on the day of her final exam. She was so sick that she couldn't concentrate, and she <u>flunked</u>! Drinking the night before a final was really stupid!*

happy hour (n) ◯ **Happy hour** takes place at some bars between approximately 5 and 8 p.m. It usually includes drinks at a discounted rate and buffet food that is usually free or inexpensive. This can be a great way to eat a cheap meal.

> *Hurry up or we'll miss **happy hour** at Happy's Bar! It's $1.99 for all-you-can-eat wings!*

heroin (n) ◯ **Heroin**, derived from the poppy plant, is a dangerous and illegal drug that is either snorted or injected. It is highly addictive. Countless people have died of heroin use. Some synonyms for **heroin** are **smack, junk,** and **dope.**

> *He was so addicted to **heroin** that he's been in <u>rehab</u> ten times.*

high (adj) ◐ Someone who is **high** is intoxicated on drugs. It can also mean to be intoxicated on alcohol, but we wouldn't suggest using the term to describe someone who is drunk, because whomever you're speaking to will probably assume that by **high** you mean drugs (which are illegal).

*Jonah was so **high** on marijuana that he crashed his car into a light pole!*

I.D. (n) ◐ You must be 21 years of age to buy or drink alcohol everywhere in the United States. **I.D.** stands for "IDentification" and refers to any official photo identification that has your birthdate on it (your student I.D. is *not* a legal proof of age). In many college towns, a person under 21 cannot even enter a liquor store or a bar.

*My favorite band is playing at the Stone Castle bar, and I can't go because I lost my **I.D.** today, and I can't prove I'm 21 without it.*

jamming (adj) ◐ When a party or concert or any social event is really good, it is **jamming.** Some synonyms are **rockin'** and **slamming.**

*That concert last night was **jamming.** I've never had such a good time before.*

joint (n) ◐ A **joint** is a marijuana cigarette. Marijuana is illegal everywhere in the United States.

*Eric smoked a **joint** with some <u>sketchy</u> guy, and he's totally <u>wasted</u>.*

jungle juice (n) ◐ Beware of **jungle juice**, a very potent concoction of fruit and grain alcohol. It is usually served out of a large cooler, in what are not the most sanitary of conditions.

*Don't drink that **jungle juice**. I think it's made from rubbing alcohol!*

keg (n) ↻ A **keg** is a large metal barrel filled with a large amount of beer, usually used for parties with a lot of people. Beer in a keg is usually cheaper than buying individual cans or bottles of beer. You need a <u>tap</u> to get the beer out of the keg.

*There are going to be about 100 people at our house tonight for the party . . . so we definitely need a **keg**.*

kegger (n) ↻ Also known as a **keg party**, a **kegger** is a party where there will be lots of people and multiple kegs of beer. Often, the host(s) of the party will charge guests for cups to help offset the cost of the beer.

*Danny just came back from the **kegger** around the corner. He said it was <u>awesome</u>, until they ran out of beer.*

kick the habit (v) ↻ A drug or alcohol addiction is called a **habit.** When a person wants to stop taking drugs and alcohol, he or she **kicks** (or gets rid of) **the habit.**

*Marissa had a really bad drug problem, but got some help, and she **kicked the habit.***

low-key (adj) ↻ When a few friends get together and just hang out and have a quiet night, it's a **low-key** night. Another word for **low-key** is **mellow.**

Woman 1: What did you do last night? Anything fun?

*Woman 2: I had fun, but it was a **low-key** night. Jared and I just stayed in and played Scrabble.*

LSD (n) ○ **LSD** is an abbreviation of Lysergic Acid Diethylamide, which is a psychotropic drug that causes hallucinations. It is illegal in the United States and considered a dangerous drug. LSD comes either in liquid form or on small pieces of paper, called tabs.

*Jackie took two tabs of **LSD**. She hallucinated and thought she could fly. Thank goodness we found her before she jumped out the window!*

OD (n) ○ **OD** is an abbreviation of OverDose. An **overdose** is when someone takes a possibly fatal dose of drugs or alcohol.

*Mark's brother died of an **OD** of <u>heroin</u>; it's so sad.*

one too many (n) ○ A person who has had **one too many** has had too much to drink. This stems from the idea that at some point while drinking, someone will have **one drink too many** and go from feeling <u>buzzed</u> to feeling sick.

*I had **one too many** beers last night. Now, I have a really bad <u>hangover</u>.*

packie (n) ○ A **packie** is a store where you can buy liquor. This term derived from **packaged goods,** which is a word for store-bought liquor.

*I'm going down to the **packie** to pick up a bottle of wine for my date with Arden.*

parlaying (v) ○ This is just a funny way to pronounce "partying."

*I spent the weekend **parlaying** and slept through my first class on Monday.*

party animal (adj) ◯ Someone who loves to go to parties and parties all of the time is a **party animal.**

*Zack is such a **party animal.** I swear I've seen him at every party I've ever been to, and he always knows where the good parties are.*

pot (n) ◯ **Pot** is the most common slang term for marijuana, which is an illegal drug derived from the marijuana plant. Some synonyms are **buds, kind bud, chronic,** and **Mary Jane.**

*If you smoke **pot,** you'll get really lazy.*

puke (v) ◯ To **puke** is to throw up, or to vomit. There are lots of slang terms for vomiting. We'll list some synonyms here: **barf, bow to the porcelain throne** (which is the toilet), **technicolor yawn, yuke, yak, heave** . . . The list goes on and on because people are continually inventing creative words for vomiting.

*I have the flu, and I was **puking** so much last night that I thought I would never stop!*

refill (n) ◯ A **refill** is when you get your drink replenished.

*Can you get me a **refill** on my soda?*

rehab (n) ◯ **Rehab** is slang for a rehabilitation center. There are many types of **rehab,** such as medical rehab after an injury and **rehab** for addiction to alcohol or drugs.

*He completed **rehab**, and he hasn't had a drop of alcohol in six months!*

roofie (n) ◯ **Roofie** is slang for Rohypnol, a drug that is used in Europe mainly as an anesthesia drug and for some other uses. It is not legal in the United States, even by prescription, so needless to say, it is a very dangerous drug. Like GHB, it has been used as a date-rape drug. You should always pay attention to your drink at a party to avoid becoming a casualty of this; if you leave a drink unattended, get a fresh one.

scene (n) ◯ The **scene** is what is happening in a certain place.

What's the scene like at the party next door? Is it rowdy or relaxed?

skinny-dipping (v) ◯ **Skinny-dipping** is swimming naked. This certainly does not happen at most parties, but it does happen. So, if someone asks you to go **skinny-dipping**, remember that you'll be nude.

Curtis and Melanie went skinny-dipping at the lake, and we stole their clothes! They had to drive home naked!

sleep it off (v) ◯ To **sleep it off** is to go to sleep after a night (or day) of drinking alcohol and wake up when sober.

Hopefully, after you've slept it off, you'll wake up feeling refreshed and rested (although you'll probably just wake up with a hangover).

spring break (n) ꙩ **Spring break** is, of course, the school vacation during the springtime when many college students go to warm beaches to party for a week, often with large groups of friends. Spring-break destinations are usually crazy and packed with people during this time. Some popular spring-break destinations in the United States are Myrtle Beach, SC; South Padre Island, TX; Daytona, FL; Virginia Beach, VA; Miami FL; and New Orleans, LA. (These are just a sampling of spring-break destinations; there are many more than we've listed, including many in Mexico.)

*I can't wait for **spring break**! I'm going to Daytona with my* <u>*roommates*</u>*, and we're going to have the best time!*

straightedge (adj) ꙩ People who are **straightedge** don't drink alcohol or do drugs.

Woman 1: Save a beer for Clarissa.

*Woman 2: She's **straightedge**; she doesn't drink that stuff.*

tap (n) ꙩ Beer cannot be released from a <u>keg</u> without a **tap,** a plastic device with a pump and a hose attached from which the beer is dispensed. **Tap** can also be used as a verb, as in "**Tap** the keg," which means "put the tap on the keg."

*Man 1: I got the keg, who has the **tap**?*

Man 2: I thought you had it?

*Man 1: Well, I don't. How are we supposed to get to the beer if we don't have a **tap**?*

tipsy (adj) ꙩ **Tipsy** means "a little bit drunk," and is usually said by or in reference to women.

*I never drink, but I had a glass of wine tonight and I feel a bit **tipsy**.*

vaca (n) ◯ This slang term is short for "vacation." It is pronounced *vay-kay.*

*I am going on **vaca** next week. South Padre Island, here I come!*

wasted (adj) ◯ Someone who is **wasted** is very intoxicated, usually from drugs, but the term can also be used to describe someone who is drunk. Some synonyms are **all <u>banged up</u>, messed up,** and **zonked.**

*Maria is totally **wasted**. She hasn't moved from that chair in 2 hours!*

4

Who's Hungry?—All about Food

In this chapter, you'll find words and phrases that describe types of food, as well as words and phrases that are derived from food terms.

apps (n) ○ **Apps** is an abbreviation of appetizers—the first course of a meal. In many bars and restaurants on college campuses, people gather and will order a lot of **apps** to share instead of individual meals.

*We ordered six **apps** for the three of us at lunch today, and now we're all too full to eat dinner.*

beef up (v) ○ This is a term that isn't about food, but refers to food. To **beef up** something is to fill it out or make it larger. Anything can be **beefed up**—from a paper (by adding text) to a person (by adding weight).

*I'm studying really hard to **beef up** my knowledge of macroeconomics so I can ace my exam tomorrow.*

BLT (n) ○ A **BLT** is a sandwich made of Bacon, Lettuce, and Tomato, often served with mayonnaise.

*I'd like a **BLT** and a <u>soda</u>, please.*

brunch (n) ○ **Brunch** is a meal that takes place between breakfast and lunch, which includes both breakfast and lunch food. **Brunch** is traditionally served on Sundays, typically between 10 a.m. and 2 p.m.

*We're going to a party tonight, and because tomorrow is Sunday, we can sleep late and still <u>hit</u> **brunch** at the dining hall.*

buffalo wings (n) ○ Buffaloes don't have wings. **Buffalo wings** are actually chicken wings that are deep fried and topped with a spicy, tobasco-based sauce. They are called **buffalo wings** because their recipe originated in Buffalo, a city in New York.

*We went to <u>happy hour</u> at Charlie's Bar, and there was so much food! I ate so many spicy **buffalo wings** that I felt like my mouth was on fire!*

caf (n) ○ **Caf** is a slang abbreviation of *cafeteria*. You may hear people refer to the dining hall as the **caf.**

Woman: Are you coming to dinner in town tonight?

*Man: No, I'm going to eat in the **caf** instead. I still have meals left on my campus meal plan.*

Canadian bacon (n) ○ **Canadian bacon** is a fried slice of ham that is usually served for breakfast.

*I'd like an egg sandwich with **Canadian bacon** instead of regular bacon, which is too greasy for me.*

chicken fingers (n) ◯ Chickens don't have fingers. **Chicken fingers** are fried strips of chicken, often served with a honey-mustard sauce. **Chicken fingers** can be found in all types of restaurants, from Italian restaurants (often on the "children's" menu) to <u>diners</u>.

*Marcy is really picky about what she eats. She hates sauces and complicated dishes, so she eats **chicken fingers** everywhere we go!*

chow (v, n) ◯ As a verb, **chow** (or **chow down**) means to eat, usually large quantities of food. As a noun, **chow** means food. So, you can **chow chow** (you can *eat food*)!

*I'm so hungry, I'm going to **chow** at the dining hall tonight—hope they have enough food!*

cola (n) ◯ **Cola** is a caramel-colored carbonated beverage, such as Coke and Pepsi. In the United States, people often use the words Coke or Pepsi to describe or ask for any kind of **cola.**

> Man: *Would you like a beverage?*
> Woman: *Sure. I'll have a **cola**, please.*

corn dog (n) ◯ A **corn dog** is a <u>hot dog</u> on a stick and covered in a fried cornmeal mix. This is a dining hall favorite—of the chef's! **Corn dogs** can also be found at places such as sporting events and food stands at parks.

> Man: *I'll have a **corn dog**.*
> Woman: *Yuck! Why would you eat a hot dog on a stick?*

dig in (v) ○ When someone tells you to **"dig in,"** you are being told to begin eating. In nonfood terms, **dig in** means to delve into or investigate something.

*Before we **dig in** to this meal, I'd like to **dig in** to finding out if you actually cooked it.*

diner (n) ○ A **diner** is a small restaurant, built to look like a railroad dining car, that has a counter along one side and booths on the other. Another definition of **diner** is a person eating dinner.

*Let's have lunch at the **diner** today. They make a great BLT!*

dish (n) ○ A **dish** is a particular kind of or variety of food, or the plate or bowl that food is served on or in. We'll give you an example of each use below.

*My favorite **dish** to order in the diner is a tuna melt.*
*Did you wash the **dishes** last night after you finished eating?*

dubious (adj) ○ **Dubious** means not trustworthy, so something that is **dubious** comes from a sketchy source. You will often hear people refer to dining-hall food as **dubious,** meaning the speaker doesn't trust the quality of the food and finds it unappetizing.

Woman 1: Are you going to eat the chicken special tonight?

*Woman 2: I don't think so, it looks pretty **dubious** to me. I'm going to stick with something safe like cereal!*

eats (n) ○ **Eats** means food. For instance, if someone says, "Let's get some **eats**," it means, "Let's go have a meal."

Man: Do you like the new restaurant in town?

*Woman: Yeah, they've got good **eats**.*

eggs Benedict (n) ◯ **Eggs Benedict** is a breakfast or <u>brunch</u> <u>dish</u>. It consists of an English muffin toasted and topped with ham, poached eggs, and hollandaise sauce.

*Would you like <u>hash browns</u> with your **eggs Benedict**?*

flapjacks (n) ◯ **Flapjacks** is a slang term for *pancakes*.

*I made **flapjacks** for breakfast yesterday, and the batter got stuck to the pan, so they all got burned.*

franks and beans (n) ◯ **Franks** is another word for <u>hot dogs</u>. **Franks and beans** is a <u>dish</u> made of chopped-up hot dogs cooked with baked beans. This is a popular <u>tailgate</u> item and is good to serve when you have to feed lots of people.

*Man 1: Do you want some **franks and beans**?*

Man 2: No, thanks. I don't like <u>hot dogs</u> or beans!

fro-yo (n) ◯ **Fro-yo** is a slang abbreviation of frozen yogurt, an ice cream-like dessert made with yogurt that is healthier than ice cream. Many dining halls have **fro-yo** machines.

*Janis is so afraid of the food in the dining hall that all she's eaten since she got to school is **fro-yo** cones with <u>sprinkles</u>.*

grease pit (n) ◯ A dingy, greasy eating establishment is a **grease pit.** This is not usually a complimentary term, but many college campuses have **grease-pit** restaurants that students are very loyal to. Some variations on this phrase are **greasy spoon** and **grease trap.**

*The Green Elbow is such a **grease pit**, but all the kids on campus hang out there for the terrific French fries.*

grease truck (n) ◯ A **grease truck** is a <u>grease pit</u> on wheels. **Grease trucks** serve <u>junk food</u> and greasy food such as hamburgers, cheese steaks, strombolis, and so on. The trucks usually park in high-traffic areas of campus.

*Josh, you really have to stop getting lunch from the **grease truck** every day . . . you've gained the <u>freshman 15</u> in two weeks!*

greens (n) ◯ **Greens** are salad vegetables, although nongreen vegetables that can be found on a salad bar still fall into the category of **greens.**

*I've eaten so much greasy food in the past week that I need to cleanse myself. So I'm eating nothing but **greens** for the next week.*

grinder (n) ◯ A **grinder** is a sandwich on a long roll, served hot in some parts of the country. This term is most often heard in the northeastern United States. Some synonyms are **submarine** and **hoagie.**

*I'd like a ham and cheese **grinder** with lettuce, tomato, and onions.*

hash browns (n) ◯ **Hash browns** are shredded or crushed potatoes that are fried and usually served to accompany breakfast.

*I'll have eggs with **hash browns**, please.*

hot dog (n) ◯ A **hot dog** is a hot frankfurter.  Some are made from beef, some are made from pork, and some are even made from chicken! **Hot dogs** are most often served on a long roll with all or any of the following condiments: ketchup, mustard, sauerkraut, onions, relish, and chili.

*May I have a **hot dog** with relish, please?*

hush puppy (n) ○ A **hush puppy** is a <u>dish</u> that is native to the South. It is a small, deep-fried cornmeal dumpling, traditionally served with fried catfish, that usually contains chopped scallions and is served hot.

*I love **hush puppies** even though I don't like to eat fried food.*

java (n) ○ **Java** is another word for coffee. Some synonyms are **joe, brew,** and **mud.**

*I stop at Joe's **Java** Shop every morning—I can't face class without a good dose of caffeine!*

junk food (n) ○ Candy, potato chips, ice cream, and other enjoyable, high-fat and/or sugar, nutritionally deficient foods are **junk foods.**

*I'm out of meal points, so I've been eating **junk food** from the vending machine. I think I've eaten three Kit-Kats today!*

mac-n-cheese (n) ○ This is a slang abbreviation for a very popular American dish: macaroni and cheese, which is elbow-shaped macaroni baked with butter, milk, and cheese. This is another dining hall staple.

*I just love **mac-n-cheese**. It's so hearty, and it reminds me of home cooking.*

mayo (n) ○ **Mayo** is an abbreviation for *mayonnaise*. You will hear mayonnaise referred to as **mayo** more often than not.

*I'll have a turkey on rye bread with lettuce, onions, and **mayo**.*

mess hall (n) ○ **Mess hall** is a military term for dining hall and is sometimes shortened to simply **mess.**

*Let's head over to the **mess hall** for dinner before all of the food is gone.*

munchies (n) ◯ When someone has the **munchies,** it means that person is in the mood to eat something (or lots of things). This term is often associated with drinking, because people who drink too much sometimes have food cravings caused by the alcohol.

*I had a bad case of the **munchies** last night, and I ate an entire big bag of chips by myself!*

nosh (v) ◯ To **nosh** means to snack. This expression is derived from the Yiddish language and has become pervasive in American society.

*The dining hall doesn't open for another two hours, so I'm going to **nosh** on some pretzels.*

PB&J (n) ◯ This is a slang abbreviation of Peanut Butter and Jelly, which is a very popular kind of sandwich in America.

*The dining hall food is so <u>gross</u> that I've eaten nothing but **PB&J** for the past five weeks!*

pig out (v) ◯ To eat a very large amount of food in one sitting is to **pig out.** This, of course, refers to the large amount of food that pigs supposedly eat.

*We left the party at midnight, and when we got home, the three of us ordered three pizzas and totally **pigged out**! There was no pizza left when we were done!*

pop (n) ◯ **Pop** is a word for a carbonated beverage of any flavor, predominantly heard in the Midwest and the South. (Also see page 130)

*He drinks so much **pop,** he should invest in the Coca-Cola company.*

rabbit food (n) ○ **Rabbit food** is a joking term for salad and vegetables, which is the kind of food rabbits eat.

I've been on a diet for three weeks, and if I have any more of that **rabbit food** *from the salad bar, I'm going to turn into a rabbit!*

scarf (v) ○ To **scarf** down food is to eat a lot of food very quickly.

I only have 15 minutes to eat lunch between classes, so I'm going to get something at the <u>grease truck</u> *and just* **scarf** *it down.*

scrapple (n) ○ **Scrapple** is a breakfast "meat" composed of scraps of other meat. Some people love **scrapple**. Try it if you will, but remember: it's *scraps*!

I can't eat breakfast with Arissa anymore; I can't stand the smell of **scrapple,** *and she eats it every day!*

seconds (n) ○ This is an abbreviation of "second serving" of food. At most dining halls, the portions are small, so you'll find yourself going for **seconds** a lot if you're hungry and you like the meal.

Tuesday is steak night at the dining hall, and you can't get **seconds** *unless everyone else has gotten their first serving.*

sling hash (v) ○ Someone who **slings hash** for a living has a job as a cook or chef. **Slinging hash** can also be a generic term for working in general.

I got a job **slinging hash** *at the local* <u>diner</u>*; I've never cooked so many eggs in my entire life!*

sloppy joe (n) ○ A **sloppy joe** is a sandwich on a hamburger roll with a ground-beef filling and a tomato-based sauce. The ground beef is loose, so the sandwich is messy, hence, sloppy. *Please note:* There are **sloppy joe** variations across the United States; in some areas, for example, if you order a **sloppy joe**, you might get roast beef, cole slaw, and thousand island dressing on bread.

*The dining hall is serving **sloppy joes** again, which really stinks, since I'm a vegetarian.*

slurp (v) ○ To **slurp** is to drink liquid in such a way that it makes a sound that sounds like "**slurp.**" **Slurp** also often denotes drinking something quickly.

*If you **slurp** down that milkshake too fast, you'll get a headache.*

so hungry I could eat a horse (v) ○ This phrase means someone is "extremely hungry."

*I haven't eaten in 12 hours, and now I'm **so hungry I could eat a horse**!*

soda (n) ○ **Soda** is any flavored, carbonated beverage. In some parts of the country, mainly the South and Midwest, soda is called **pop**. Low-calorie soda is called **diet soda.**

*I'll have a hamburger and a **soda**.*

SOS (n) ○ **SOS** is an abbreviation of the military slang term S - - - On a Shingle (s - - - is a curse word that we have not filled in, you know what we mean), which is *creamed chipped corn beef* (shredded corn beef in a cream sauce). Like scrapple, this is an acquired taste.

*I'll have two eggs and a side of **SOS**.*

spreads (n) ○ **Spreads** refer to any kind of food that can be spread on crackers or chips. Some examples of spreads are spinach dip, crab dip, sour cream and onion dip, and so on.

*We were expecting twenty people to <u>tailgate</u> with us at the football game, so we made a bunch of **spreads** for appetizers.*

sprinkles (n) ○ **Sprinkles** are chocolate or candy chips used as an ice-cream topping. You will probably find them right next to the <u>fro-yo</u> machine in the <u>mess</u>. In some regions of the United States, people refer to **sprinkles** as **Jimmies**.

*I'll have chocolate ice cream in a cone with chocolate **sprinkles**, please.*

stuff your face (v) ○ To **stuff your face** is to eat too much, usually too fast. This is an allusion to literally stuffing, or forcing, food into one's mouth.

*He **stuffed his face** with crab legs at the party, and he drank way too much, so it's no wonder he <u>puked</u>.*

stuffed (adj) ○ If you are **stuffed,** you are too full—you have eaten too much, maybe to the point of sickness.

*I'm so **stuffed**. I ate six slices of pizza.*

sunny-side up eggs (n) ○ **Sunny-side up eggs** are fried eggs served rare with the yolks intact. A variation on this is **eggs over easy,** which are fried eggs turned over once to cook the yolks a little more but still served with the yolks intact.

*I'll have two **sunny-side up eggs** with bacon.*

swill (n) ○ **Swill** describes any distasteful beverage, and it is sometimes used to describe distasteful food.

*This dining hall serves nothing but **swill**! It's so unhealthy.*

tater (n) ○ **Tater** is a slang term for any kind of potato—mashed, French fries, hash browns, and so on.

*I won't eat the meat in the dining hall, so I have whatever kind of **taters** are available.*

tip (n) ○ A **tip** is a gratuity left for a server at a restaurant. In the United States, the **tip** is not usually included in the restaurant bill as it is in some parts of Europe, unless the party is composed of more than five people. A traditional tip is at least 15 percent of the total bill for good service.

*I waited tables for 3 hours this morning and only made $2 in **tips**.*

veggies (n) ○ **Veggies** are vegetables.

*I only eat **veggies**, no meat.*

wash down (v) ○ To **wash down** food is to drink a beverage after swallowing the food.

*He **washed down** a tuna sandwich with a soda.*

5

You Can Count on It—Money, Numbers, Shopping, and Time

It's no surprise that many slang terms and idioms refer to numbers, because numbers play such a large role in life. Time and money are related to numbers, and shopping is related to money, which is how we've come up with the words included in this chapter. You probably can't count the number of times in a day you use numbers or numerical references. (See? We just used one!) After you read the words in this chapter, think about all of the expressions in your native language that deal with money and numbers—we think you'll find that there are a lot of them.

5-finger discount (n) ○ **5-finger discount** is slang for shoplifting (stealing merchandise from a store), referring to stealing with your hands.

> *Woman 1: Where did you get that great bracelet, Nancy? I thought you had no money.*
>
> *Woman 2: I used the **5-finger discount** down at the store, so it didn't cost me a thing!*
>
> *Woman 1: That's illegal, you know. You could get in trouble!*

a blank check (n) ○ When someone gives someone else the chance to do something with no restrictions, it is called giving that person **a blank check.** This is a reference to the opportunity a blank check would present—you could write it out for as much money as you want.

*Professor Jordan basically gave me **a blank check** when it came to choosing a topic for my term paper; he said I could write about absolutely anything, so I'm writing about my favorite thing—food!*

ahead of time (adv) ○ When you do something in advance of or in preparation for something else, you have done it **ahead of time.**

*I have a paper due tomorrow for English composition class, but I finished it and handed it in **ahead of time** so I can hang out with my friends tonight.*

an arm and a leg (adv) ○ A very expensive item or service is said to cost an **arm and a leg.** In other words, the item is so expensive that paying for it feels like you are chopping off one of your arms and one of your legs to pay.

*Dan's parents bought him the new Beemer convertible. It must have cost **an arm and a leg.** They could have saved some cash if they got him a less expensive car.*

astronomical (adj) ○ This refers to something with a very high price. It is usually used in terms of things such as rent and fees such as school tuition.

*I'm going to a state college. I wanted to go to that private art school in the city, but the tuition is so **astronomical** that I'd be paying off my student loans for the next forty years!*

bank (n) ◯ As a noun, **bank** means "a lot of money." Some synonyms are **dough** and **duckets.** Remember, this is the slang usage, which is derived from the traditional meaning of the word **bank,** which is a building or organization that safeguards money.

*Jim is a successful businessman; he's got a lot of **bank,** so he buys his girlfriend lots of expensive stuff and only eats at the best restaurants. I wish I had the **bank** for that; but, hey, some people seem to have all the **dough** and the rest of us have none.*

bank (adj) ◯ As an adjective, **bank** means something or someone that can be counted on or trusted.

*My roommate knows a huge secret about me, but she's **bank,** so she'll never tell anyone else.*

bank on it ◯ (v) If you can be sure that something will happen, then you can **bank on it,** which refers to the reliability of banks. This phrase is not usually applied to people, but to situations.

Man 1: Are you sure you can pick me up from the football game on Sunday?

*Man 2: You can **bank on it**. I always keep my promises.*

benjamins (n) ◯ Benjamin Franklin's picture is printed on the American $100 bill, which is where the expression **benjamins** is derived from. When something is said to be "all about the **benjamins,**" it means it's all about the money.

*I really hate my job working in the dining hall, but, hey, it's all about the **benjamins**—I have to work to pay my tuition so I can stay in school.*

biggie (n) ◯ The most common use of **biggie** is as a noun, to mean a big favor. This comes from the word *big*, meaning large in size. Something can also be said to be **no biggie,** which means that it is "not a big problem."

> *Woman 1: Suzanne, I need to ask you a **biggie**. Can you help me write my term paper? It needs to be sixty pages long, and it's due tomorrow.*
>
> *Woman 2: Sure I can help; it's no **biggie**. I have no plans for tonight anyway.*

blow (v) ◯ To **blow** all of your money means to spend all of your money, usually very quickly and on something that is unnecessary.

> *I'm going to Las Vegas on spring break. I'm going to try not to **blow** all my money gambling like I did last time—I came home totally <u>broke</u>!*

bread (n) ◯ This is used as a generic term to refer to money and is not specific to a large or small amount. A synonym is **cash.**

> *Man 1: Do you want to come to dinner in town with us?*
>
> *Man 2: I can't. I've got no **bread**. I don't get paid until tomorrow.*
>
> *Man 1: I can lend you some cash and you can <u>pay back</u> the money tomorrow.*

bring home the bacon (v) ◯ The phrase "to **bring home the bacon**" has nothing to do with food. It means to make money.

> *I got a really great job at a telemarketing agency! I'll really be **bringing home the bacon** now, so I won't have to borrow money from you all the time!*

broke (adj) ↻ If someone has absolutely no money, that person is said to be **broke.** You'll probably hear this a lot around campus.

*It would be so awesome to go on the bus trip to New York City for the day with my <u>dorm</u>, but I'm **broke,** so I can't afford the bus ticket.*

bucks (n) ↻ Perhaps the most common slang term dealing with money, **bucks** means dollars.

Man 1: How much did your bike cost?
*Man 2: One hundred fifty **bucks.***

buck up (v) ↻ To **buck up** is to pay for something. This is usually used in situations when a group of people are paying for something, such as beer or dinner. When the check comes, everyone has to **buck up,** or pay.

*I'm picking up the <u>keg</u> from the liquor store now, and I need to leave a $20 deposit. I only have five <u>bucks</u>, so the rest of you guys have to **buck up** now.*

buy time (v) ↻ If you need more time to complete your take-home final, you may need to **buy time,** which means to figure out how to get more time to complete your task, even if it means inventing an excuse. Needing to **buy time** implies a situation that is stressful.

*I'm avoiding telling Becky that I've been seeing another girl. I think I can **buy some time** to think of a good excuse by avoiding her phone calls and e-mails.*

cheap (adj) ◯ Cheap means "not expensive." Something that is cheap can be good, such as used books at the bookstore. Cheap can also be used to describe a thing or a person in a negative way.

*The used books at the bookstore are so much **cheaper** than the new books, and they both have the same content! So used books are a good value.*

*I hate this <u>dorm</u> furniture. It's so **cheap** looking and <u>gross</u>—it will probably fall apart two months into the semester.*

checkout (n) ◯ The cash register in a store where you pay for your merchandise before you leave is called a **checkout,** usually used in terms of a supermarket.

*It's supposed to snow tomorrow, and the **checkout** line at the supermarket was so long I thought I'd never get to pay for my groceries and get home before the snow got too bad!*

cheese (n) ◯ This is yet another term for money and is used in very informal situations. You would never use the word **cheese** when speaking to one of your professors, but it's acceptable for use with your friends.

*Andrew's parents are very wealthy, and he's always got the **cheese** to go out and party all night. Me? I'm **cheese**-free right now, without even a couple of dollars for a single beer.*

clean up (n) ◯ To **clean up** is to make a lot of money on something, usually quickly.

*I sold back my books to the student bookstore today, and I really **cleaned up.** I got $150 for last semester's books—I only got $45 the year before!*

cough up (v) ○ This phrase is similar in meaning to <u>buck up,</u> but it is not used as a command. When you need to **cough up** cash for something, it means that you have to pay for something that you'd rather not pay for.

*My <u>roommate</u> dropped out of school, and now I have to **cough up** the cash to cover her part of our rent!*

count on (something) (v) ○ When you can **count on** something, it means that you can trust that it will happen. This is similar to <u>bank on</u> but **count on** is usually used when referring to people as opposed to situations.

*Sheila is my best friend. I can always **count on** her to help me out in a tough situation.*

crack of dawn (n) ○ The **crack of dawn** is literally the first light of the morning when the sun rises. This expression is not always used to indicate the actual beginning of the morning. For someone who likes to sleep late (like some college students), noon is considered the **crack of dawn!**

*Woman 1: I have to get home and go to sleep—my first class tomorrow is at the **crack of dawn!***

*Woman 2: Are you <u>kidding</u> me? Your first class is at 1 p.m.! My first class is at 7 a.m. Now, that's the **crack of dawn!***

damage (n) ○ The **damage** is the final total that you pay for something . . . usually said when shopping or as a way of asking someone what he or she paid for something.

Woman 1: May I <u>ring up</u> your purchases?

*Woman 2: Thanks. What's the **damage**? I hope I didn't spend more than $200.*

deep pockets (adj) ○ Someone who has **deep pockets** has a lot of money to spend. This term can also be applied to institutions, such as schools or corporations.

> Man 1: *Do you really think that the lawsuit against XYZ Company will be successful?*
>
> Man 2: *No. XYZ has really **deep pockets**, so it can afford to pay lawyers anything they want . . . it'll never run out of money!*

dinero (n) ○ This is the Spanish word for money, but it has been adopted into American English, and means money in English as well. Unlike <u>bucks</u>, **dinero** refers to a sum of money, not to individual dollars.

> *I hope you have a lot of **dinero**, because the price to see a movie just went up from $7.50 to $11.00!*

dirt cheap (adj, adv) ○ This is a term you will hear in conjunction with shopping or when someone is talking about a purchase. Something that is **dirt cheap** is very inexpensive, but not in a negative way. Usually, when someone tells you they got something **dirt cheap**, that person is saying he or she got a good deal or paid a low price on something that usually costs more.

> Woman 1: *What a great purse!*
>
> Woman 2: *Thanks. I got it **dirt cheap** at a <u>yard sale</u> this weekend. It would have cost me twice as much at the <u>mall</u>!*

drag on (v) ○ This expression is used to refer to time that seems to be moving very slowly. So, even though time cannot really move any faster or more slowly than it does, a really boring class can seem to **drag on** forever, making 60 minutes seem more like 600 minutes.

*My economics class **dragged on and on** today . . . I really thought the professor would never stop talking! I thought I was going to be late for my next class until I looked at the clock and realized there were still 10 minutes to go in this one!*

fat cat (n) ○ Someone who has a lot of money and is very powerful is a **fat cat.** This term is often used to describe executives in large companies.

*I don't want to become a corporate **fat cat**, so I'm devoting my life to charity work.*

flow (n) ○ This is yet another word for cash, but **flow** usually refers to a wage or money made from a job.

*Now that I got a job at the local clothes store, I've got plenty of **flow** to go out and party this weekend and whenever else I want to.*

foot the bill (v) ○ When you **foot the bill,** you pay for something. This phrase is often used when a person or an organization is paying not just for themselves, but for others as well.

*I don't have to worry about paying housing costs for my <u>dorm</u> room, because I'm an <u>RA</u> and the school **foots the bill.***

freebie (n) ◯ A **freebie** is something that is free (costs nothing). Getting a **freebie** is a good thing.

> Man 1: *Where did you get that great hat?*
>
> Man 2: *It was a **freebie**. The record store is giving them away when you sign up for the mailing list.*

funny money (n) ◯ Fake, or counterfeit, money is called **funny money.** A synonym for this is **monopoly money,** so called because of the fake money that comes with the Monopoly game.

> Man 1: *Dude, you owe me $20, and don't give me any **funny money**.*
>
> Man 2: *Hey man, I'm not giving you fake cash! I've got bank.*

good deal (n) ◯ When you get something for a good price, it's a **good deal.** This term is also sometimes used to indicate something that is good in general, not necessarily in terms of a purchase, and can also indicate a large amount of something.

> *Dave got three cases of Ramen noodles for $5. At 20 noodle cups a case, he got a **good deal** of noodles in a really **good deal.***

got bills? (v) ◯ This expression means "do you have money?" It is derived from the advertising campaign slogan for America's Dairy Farmers and Milk Processors—Got Milk?

> Man 1: ***Got bills?***
>
> Man 2: *Nah, I'm broke.*

grand (n) ◯ A **grand** is $1,000, five **grand** is $5,000, and so on.

> *It cost me three **grand** to fix my car!*

gravy train (n) ꙩ The **gravy train** refers to money that someone gets that is unearned or undeserved; in a less mean sense, it means someone's financial support.

*Her husband is her **gravy train**. He works all day, and she sits at home and does nothing!*

hush money (n) ꙩ **Hush money** is money paid to keep someone from talking about something.

Woman 1: Jennie settled her dispute with XYZ company.

*Woman 2: Yeah, she got twenty grand in **hush money;** she's not allowed to talk about the case to anyone else ever.*

K (n) ꙩ Like a grand, **K** means $1,000, but **K** is usually used in terms of salary.

*I make 150**K** a year working for a prominent law firm.*

laughing all the way to the bank (v) ꙩ If you do something that no one else expects to be successful and you are successful, it is said that you are **laughing all the way to the bank**—you are laughing because you had detractors and you are very happy that you were successful.

Woman 1: My roommate wrote the dumbest thesis ever! She doesn't deserve a good grade on it.

*Woman 2: Well, she got an A+ on that thesis, so she's **laughing all the way to the bank.***

layaway (n) ❍ This is a term strictly applied to shopping. When you put something on **layaway,** the store holds it for you and you pay for it in installments. When you have paid the whole amount, you collect the merchandise from the store and it's yours.

I can't afford a new computer, but Computer City has a great **layaway** *plan. I just pay ten* <u>bucks</u> *a month and in ten months, the computer is mine!*

living hand to mouth (v) ❍ When you are **living hand to mouth**, you are spending your money as it comes in and not saving any because you can't afford to save. Another way to say this is **living from paycheck to paycheck.**

Joe lost his job, so he and his wife are **living hand to mouth**—*it's a really tough situation.*

mall (n) ❍ This is a large building filled with all sorts of specialty stores, so it's a place where you can find all sorts of things, from clothing to toys. (See Chapter 1 for an alternate definition of **mall**.) (Also see page 13)

You'll find what you need at the **mall.** *There are so many stores there.*

marry into money (v) ❍ When you marry someone who is wealthy, you have **married into money.**

Angie grew up poor, and she used to be so nice. But she **married into money,** *and now she acts like she's better than everyone else!*

maxed-out (adj) ◯ This term is used mainly in reference to credit cards. When you are **maxed out,** it means that you have spent your whole credit limit. For instance, if your credit-card limit is $5,000 and you have spent $5,000, you no longer have any money left. This phrase is also sometimes used to indicate being exhausted.

*I can't afford to buy my books for this semester yet. I'm totally **maxed out** on my credit card, and I can't spend any more on it until I make a payment, and I have no* <u>bucks</u>. *What am I going to do?*

megabucks (n) ◯ *Mega* means large, so **megabucks** means "a large amount of money."

*Michele's new Porsche cost **megabucks,** but that's okay—she has **megabucks** to spend.*

paid off (v) ◯ When you do something that is lucrative or successful, you say that it **paid off.**

*All that exercise really **paid off.** You look great!*

pass the buck (v) ◯ To **pass the buck** is to pass the responsibility for something on to someone else.

*I was supposed to do one quarter of our group project for history class, but I got sick, so I **passed the buck** to someone else in the group and she did the work for me.*

pay back (v) ◯ If you borrow money from someone else or from a bank, you have to **pay it back,** which means you **pay back** the money that you owe.

*Jimmy loaned me $50 last night for my date with Sarah. I have to **pay him back** as soon as I get some cash.*

pay off (v) ⟲ This term is usually used in reference to a loan of money, such as a car loan. You **pay off** a loan in installments.

*I'll be **paying off** my student loans for thirty years!*

payoff (n) ⟲ When used as a noun, a **payoff** is money taken to keep quiet about something.

*She took a **payoff** from her <u>bookie</u> and refused to testify against him at trial.*

peanuts (n) ⟲ **Peanuts** means a little bit of money or something that is low cost.

*I make **peanuts** at my job compared to my <u>roommate</u> who makes a lot of money.*

plastic (n) ⟲ A credit card is called ***plastic.***

*I've got no cash on me, but luckily, I have **plastic,** so I can just charge it.*

red cent (n) ⟲ This phrase is usually used when someone refuses to pay for something, usually preceded by the word *not*. A synonym is **not one red penny.**

*I will not pay that cab driver one **red cent!** He almost killed me on the ride home!*

ring (someone) **up** (v) ◯ This term applies to shopping. When a shopkeeper totals the price of a purchase on the cash register, she **rings you up.**

> Woman 1: *Did you find everything you need in the store?*
>
> Woman 2: *Yes, thanks.*
>
> Woman 1: *Why don't you step over to the cash register then, and I'll* **ring you up?**

rip-off (n, v) ◯ A **rip-off** is something that is priced much higher than it is worth. Someone who sells you something that is not worth what you paid has **ripped you off.** This term can also denote anything that is unfair.

> *This blouse is such a* **rip-off.** *I saw it in a store across the street for $10 less!*

sale (n, v) ◯ A **sale** is when a store offers its merchandise at a discounted price. This word can be used as part of a verb phrase, **on sale,** as in "something is **on sale.**"

> *They are having a* **sale** *at my favorite store, and I got a great sweater for 50 percent off.*

save coin (v) ◯ To **save coin** is to save money. *Coin* is another slang term for money.

> *I really need to* **save some coin** *if I want to go to Cancun on spring break.*

shell out (v) ◯ To spend money for something or to pay for something is to **shell out** money.

> *I have to* **shell out** *$500 for my meal plan this semester, now that they've instituted a minimum balance. Last year, I had to pay only $300.*

slush fund (n) ○ A **slush fund** is money saved for use either in an emergency or for recreation.

*I shouldn't be able to afford that summer trip to Europe, but I have a secret **slush fund**, and I'm going to use it to pay for the trip!*

splurge (n, v) ○ When used as a noun, **splurge** means to spend money on a luxury or unnecessary item. **Splurge** can also be used as a verb, as in "to splurge on something."

*I'm supposed to be saving my money, but I **splurged** and had lunch at a good restaurant instead of at the dining hall.*

stash (n, v) ○ As a noun, a **stash** is a secret store of money. As a verb, it means to put money away to save.

*I've been **stashing away** money all semester so that I can buy a ticket to Aspen to ski during winter break.*

strapped for cash (adj) ○ When someone is **strapped for cash,** that person is lacking money.

Man 1: Are you coming to the bar tonight?
*Man 2: No, I'm too **strapped for cash** right now.*

under the mattress (adv) ○ Someone who doesn't trust banks is said to keep money **under the mattress.**

*I keep my money **under the mattress** because I don't want to pay banking fees, and I want my money to be close to me.*

wad (n) ○ A **wad** is a roll of bills and usually refers to money carried by a man (women tend to use wallets more often, we think).

*When it was time to <u>foot the bill</u>, Larry pulled out a **wad** of twenties.*

yard sale (n) ○ A **yard sale** is the sale of household items and clothing by the original owners, usually set up in a yard or garage. *Please note:* In some areas of the country, it is known as a *tag sale.*

*We cleaned out the attic, so we're going to have a **yard sale** to get rid of the stuff we don't need anymore.*

zip (n) ○ **Zip** means "zero" or "nothing." A synonym is **zilch.**

Man 1: You have nothing left?
*Man 2: That's correct. I have **zip**.*

6

Let's Get Emotional—People and Their Feelings

In this chapter, you will find words and phrases that describe types of people and emotions. And believe us, there are lots of different people on college campuses and lots of emotions floating around as well!

ag (adj) ○ **Ag** is a slang abbreviation of "aggravated," which means annoyed.

*I get so **ag** when my <u>roommate</u> goes on and on about her <u>boyfriend</u>.*

a'ight (adj) ○ This has become a very popular expression in recent years. It is a contraction of "all right," meaning, "just fine." It is pronounced *ah-ITE*, and rhymes with tight and might.

Woman: How are you doing?

*Man: I'm **a'ight**. Can't complain.*

bad egg (adj) ↻ A **bad egg** is a bad person who is bad by nature and can't be changed. The opposite of a **bad egg** is a **good egg**; however, the expression **good egg** is somewhat dated.

*My <u>roommate</u> is just a **bad egg.** She doesn't even try to be nice to people, and she has no respect for anything or anyone.*

beat (adv) ↻ Someone who is **beat** is exhausted. You'll hear this expression often, especially around exam time.

*I'm so **beat** because I've been up studying all night. I haven't slept at all!*

big shot (adj) ↻ A **big shot** is an important and powerful person.

*That boy thinks he's such a **big shot** because he's president of the student body, but I think he's a <u>jerk</u>.*

bleeding heart (adj) ↻ A **bleeding heart** is an extremely liberal person (the word "liberal" is most often attached to **bleeding heart**).

*I'm a member of the young Republicans, but my <u>roommate</u> is a complete **bleeding heart** liberal. So, we have an agreement not to talk about politics so that we don't fight with each other!*

blip (n) ↻ A **blip** is an unimportant person. This refers to **blips** on a radar screen, which are small and unimportant/momentary things. This is not a nice thing to say about someone.

Man 1: Who is this girl that you like? I've never seen her before.

*Man 2: She's some **blip**. I never would have noticed her, but we're paired together for a project in class. I'm glad I got to meet her.*

blue (adv) ❍ To feel **blue** is to feel sad or depressed.

*Joe has been feeling really **blue** since his <u>girlfriend</u> <u>broke up</u> with him.*

BMOC (n) ❍ **BMOC** is an acronym for Big Man On Campus, which means a very popular man. This term is fairly dated, but you may hear it used from time to time, especially in a sarcastic manner.

*That boy is so <u>full of</u> himself! Does he think he's the **BMOC** because he was crowned <u>homecoming king</u>?*

bug out (v, adj) ❍ To **bug out** is to panic. This term is often used in reference to people who are on drugs or alcohol and experiencing panic. **Bug out** can also be used as an adjective to describe a panic-filled situation or a situation that causes one to <u>freak out</u>.

*This party is a huge **bug out**! I can't deal with all of these people and the loud music—let's get out of here.*

bummed out (adv) ❍ To be **bummed out** is to be disappointed or sad about something. A bad or disappointing situation is a **bummer.**

*I was supposed to go to the homecoming dance with Bruce tonight, but he canceled. I'm so **bummed out** about it because I really wanted to go.*

can't stand (v) ❍ If you **can't stand** someone, it means that you hate that person and can't tolerate being around him or her. This very common expression also applies to objects.

*I **can't stand** my <u>RA</u>. She's too cheery for me; I don't trust people who smile all the time.*

catty (adj) ↺ Someone who is **catty** is not nice or trustworthy. For instance, a **catty** person would make hurtful remarks to someone or would gossip behind someone's back.

*She's so **catty**—I can't think of one person about whom she has something nice to say!*

copycat (n) ↺ A **copycat** is someone who copies everything someone else does.

*My roommate is such a **copycat**. Every time I buy something new, she goes out and buys the same thing.*

crazy about (v) ↺ To be **crazy about** something or someone is to love it (or him or her). If you don't like something, you can say you're "not **crazy about** it."*

*He's **crazy about** basketball. He does nothing else during basketball season but watch games on television.*

dense (adj) ↺ **Dense** means thick. As a slang term, it means a person who is not smart.

*Why are you so **dense**? This is a simple topic, and you can't understand it.*

draw a blank (v) ↺ To **draw a blank** is to forget something. This is an allusion to trying to call up a piece of information in your head and "seeing" only a blank piece of paper.

*I'm sorry, I'm **drawing a blank** trying to remember your name. What is it again?*

dude (n) ◯ A **dude** is a man or a woman. Many people will address everyone as "dude." **Dude** can also be used as a question, meaning "can you repeat that" or "what did you just say?" In fact, some people believe that **dude** can be used to substitute any word in the English language!

> Man 1: **Dude,** *did you do the chemistry homework?*
>
> Man 2: **Dude?**
>
> Man 1: *I said,* **Dude,** *did you do the chemistry homework?*

dying for (v) ◯ If you must have something, you say you are **dying for** it.

> *It's so hot that I'm* **dying for** *an iced tea.*

fair-weather friend (n) ◯ A **fair-weather friend** is a person who is only friends with you when times are good. You can't count on a **fair-weather friend** to help you out in bad times.

> *Rhonda is such a* **fair-weather friend.** *The second I broke up with Bobby, she wouldn't hang out with me. She says she only likes cheery people.*

flake (n) ◯ A **flake** is a forgetful and/or untrustworthy person. To **flake out** is to forget something.

> *She's such a* **flake!** *She forgot to feed her fish for a week and they died!*

freak out (v) ◯ To **freak out** is to lose your cool or temper.

> *I* **freaked out** *when I found out that I failed my final! My parents are going to be so upset.*

full of it (adj) ◯ Someone who is **full of it** pretends to know all about something he or she really does not know anything about. This expression can also mean someone is a liar.

*You're so **full of it**! How can you say you didn't steal my toothbrush when I saw you do it?*

full of oneself (adj) ◯ People who are **full of themselves** are conceited or self-centered.

*My professor is so **full of himself**! He thinks he's the best professor to ever walk the Earth.*

get over it (v) ◯ If you are no longer upset about something that has happened to you, you have **gotten over it.** So, if someone tells you to **get over** something, that person is telling you to stop being upset or concerned about it.

Man 1: I can't believe Emily <u>broke up</u> with me!
*Man 2: **Get over it.** There are other women out there to date.*

girly girl (n) ◯ A **girly girl** is a girl who likes very feminine things and avoids manly or messy things.

*I don't think Hanna will go camping with us. She's too much of a **girly girl,** so there's no way she's sleeping in a tent.*

go-getter (n) ꙩ A **go-getter** is a person who is enthusiastic and works hard to go after the things he or she wants. This implies a person who takes a great deal of personal initiative in everything he or she does.

*Max is a real **go-getter.** He couldn't get into the class that he wanted, so he began to attend the class anyway and finally convinced the professor to let him take the class, even though it was full.*

green with envy (adj) ꙩ Someone who is **green with envy** is very jealous. Jealousy is sometimes referred to as "the green-eyed monster."

*I can't believe you got an A in Psych 101! I took it last year and barely passed! I'm **green with envy!***

hard feelings (n) ꙩ **Hard feelings** are bad feelings between two people. When two people who have been in a fight make up, they may say "no **hard feelings,**" meaning, we harbor no ill will toward one another.

*She has really **hard feelings** about the boy who broke her heart.*

head is spinning (v) ꙩ If your **head is spinning,** you have received so much information in a small period of time that you can't think straight—in other words, you feel like your head is actually spinning.

*I just finished listening to a 2-hour lecture on microeconomics, and my **head is spinning.***

hippie (n) ○ A **hippie** is someone who rejects (or is in opposition to) many conventional standards and customs of society. Many **hippies** are in favor of extreme liberalism in lifestyle and politics. This term can also be used to describe fans of The Grateful Dead, Phish, and other bands of that genre, regardless of the political views of those fans. This term became popular in the 1960s. (Also see page 103)

*You're such a **hippie** that you should go live on a commune and start your own society, because your views are more liberal than any I've ever heard!*

in a tizzy (v) ○ Someone who is **in a tizzy** is confused and flustered.

*Don't get yourself all **in a tizzy**! We have a week to finish this project, so just relax!*

jerk (n) ○ A **jerk** is a person who is not nice—or downright mean and rude.

*He's such a **jerk** because he never called when he said he would.*

joe (adj) ○ **Joe** means "average" or "in general" and is derived from the term "average **joe**." So, if you say, "he's a **joe** boy," you mean "he's an average boy."

***Joe** audience member will never notice if you mess up your lines on stage if you're quick to cover it up; only experienced theater people would notice that.*

kidding (v) ○ **Kidding** means "joking."

Woman: I can't believe you said that mean thing to me!

*Man: Don't be mad! I was just **kidding**. I didn't mean it!*

know it all (n) ○ A person who thinks he or she knows everything about everything and shares this "knowledge" with everyone to the point of being annoying is a **know it all.**

*You're such a **know it all**! You think you know more than the professor!*

loser (n) ○ A **loser** is an uncool person, that is, someone who is not popular. Some synonyms are **nerd, geek,** and **dweeb.** This is not a nice thing to call someone; however, friends will sometimes call each other these names as a joke.

*Gosh! You're such a **loser**! Do you ever do anything else besides study?*

lost (one's) ***marbles*** (v) ○ Someone who has **lost his or her marbles** has gone crazy or is acting irrationally.

*My <u>roommate</u> has really **lost his marbles**. He was speaking to himself last night!*

mellow (adj) ○ **Mellow** means "calm and relaxed." A person, place, or situation can be described as **mellow.** A synonym is **low-key.**

*That <u>dude</u> is so **mellow**. He never gets upset about anything!*

out of it (v) ○ To be **out of it** is to be confused and not involved with what is going on around you. A person who is on drugs or is drunk is often described as being **out of it.**

*I am so worried about my finals that I haven't slept in a week. I feel really **out of it** today.*

out on a limb (v) ○ To go **out on a limb** for someone or something is to take a chance for that person or thing.

*I'm not going to put myself **out on a limb** to help her with this project. I have to be selfish and think about protecting myself before I help her.*

over (one's) ***head*** (v) ○ If something that is said goes **over someone's head,** it means the person does not understand it. This expression is often heard after a person tells a joke to someone else—if the other person does not "get" or understand the joke, it has gone **over his or her head.**

*My advanced theory class was way **over my head,** so I dropped it and picked up an easier class.*

perfect stranger (n) ○ This is a somewhat odd expression. A **stranger** is someone you don't know. Somewhere in the evolution of the English language, the word **perfect** became part of the expression, so a **perfect stranger** is someone you don't know.

*I'm not going on a date with a **perfect stranger**! I have to meet a person before I will date him.*

pissed off (v) ○ **Pissed off** means angry. Sometimes people just say **pissed** without "off"—it means the same thing. This term is so common that you will probably hear it within 5 minutes of being on campus for the first time. A synonym is **ticked off.**

*My roommate drank the last of the milk and I'm **pissed off** because now I have to drink my coffee black!*

pooped (v) ○ **Pooped** means "extremely tired." This can sound like a strange expression to you if you know that "poop" is a word for excrement. However, although poop and **pooped** sound a lot alike, they have very different meanings.

*I partied until dawn yesterday, and now I'm totally **pooped**!*

pushy (adj) ○ A person who is **pushy** bosses around other people. It's good to be a go-getter but not to be **pushy,** because **pushy** people make other people uncomfortable.

*This guy on my project team for history is so **pushy**! Everyone else in the group wanted to report on the role of women in World War II, but he insisted that we do the project on the role of cats in World War II.*

second thoughts (n) ○ When you are unsure that you have made a correct decision about something, you are having **second thoughts.**

*I'm having **second thoughts** about majoring in political science. I wish I majored in fine arts instead.*

skitzing (v) ○ **Skitzing** is being very nervous about a situation and losing your ability to reason.

*My parents are totally **skitzing** about the ski trip I'm going on. They don't want me to go because they think I'll get hurt.*

slacker (n) ○ A **slacker** is a lazy person who does no work, school or otherwise. This term sometimes denotes someone who is lazy and smokes marijuana.

*My boyfriend's roommate could be a professional **slacker**. I've never seen anyone work so hard at doing nothing!*

take advantage of (v) ○ To **take advantage of** something is to get the best results out of it that you can for yourself. To **take advantage of** people is to cheat them or make them do something they don't want to do because they don't know any better.

*You should **take advantage of** the free meal week at the dining hall so you can save money. But don't **take advantage** of the servers by taking seconds when you're not allowed to.*

the man (n) ○ Someone who is **the man** is "the best." This term usually applies to men, but it has become so common that it can also be used to refer to women. This is often heard in the expression "you *da* man," with *da* replacing "the."

> Man: *I got those concert tickets.*
>
> *Woman: You da **man**! I thought the concert was sold out!*

tongue-tied (adj) ○ People who are **tongue-tied** cannot think of anything to say or cannot say what they are thinking correctly, usually because they are surprised.

*The professor called on me in class for the first time, and I was so **tongue-tied** that I couldn't say the correct answer, even though I knew it.*

tree hugger (n) ○ This is a name, sometimes meant in a derogatory manner, for an environmentalist.

*Warren is a true **tree hugger**. He yells at anyone who is not so environmentally concerned as he is.*

trippin (v) ○ Someone who is **trippin** is freaking out or very upset or worried about something.

*My <u>rents</u> were totally **trippin** when I told them I was going on an overnight ski trip with my friends. They really worry too much!*

under the weather (adv) ○ When you feel **under the weather,** you feel sick.

*I'm feeling a little bit **under the weather** today, so I made a doctor's appointment.*

waiter (n) ○ A **waiter** is a male server in a restaurant. A **waitress** is a female server.

*Can you ask the **waiter** for the bill, please?*

wuss (n) ○ A **wuss** is a person who is weak of will and who backs down when confronted by someone.

*Just talk to her! Don't be such a **wuss**!*

yuppie (n) ○ A **yuppie** is a Young Urban Professional. This term became popular in the 1980s.

*He's such a **yuppie**. He drives a <u>Beemer</u> and is president of his company—and he's only 23.*

7

Lookin' Good—Clothing and Appearance

Appearance is important to many people. In college, many students find themselves free for the first time to develop and express their personal styles. In this chapter, you'll find words and phrases about types of clothing and about the way people look.

all that (adj) ◯ Someone who is **all that** is attractive and well dressed. This is a very high compliment. (Also see page 162)

*That girl is **all that**. I've had a <u>crush</u> on her since September.*

bad hair day (n) ◯ A **bad hair day** is a day when your hair looks bad. This term is also used commonly to describe any bad day, regardless of how one's hair looks.

*I'm having such a **bad hair day**. Besides the fact that my hair is a mess, I think I <u>flunked</u> my final!*

belly chain (n) ◯ A **belly chain** is a chain of silver or gold worn around the waist and sometimes strung through a belly-button ring (most commonly worn by girls).

*That **belly chain** looks really nice with your <u>belly shirt</u>.*

belly shirt (n) ◯ A **belly shirt** is a shirt usually worn by girls that exposes the midriff—often worn with low-waisted pants.

*That **belly shirt** is not an appropriate thing to wear for our group presentation in class. You should change into something more modest.*

black-tie (adj) ◯ **Black-tie** refers to a tuxedo. A **black-tie** affair is one in which formal wear for women and tuxedos for men are the required attire.

*The Kappa Kappa Alpha <u>formal</u> is **black-tie** this year, so all of the <u>brothers</u> rented tuxes.*

bling-bling (n) ◯ **Bling-bling** is shiny, extravagant jewelry.

*Nice **bling-bling**. I'm blinded by all of the sparkling stones.*

bundle up (v) ◯ To **bundle up** is to put on many layers of clothing to go out in very cold weather. Those of you attending school in the Northeast, Northwest, or Midwest will hear this term often during the cold winters.

*There's a blizzard outside. You better **bundle up** before you walk to class or you'll be freezing.*

busted (adj) ◯ To look **busted** is to look really bad, tired, and/or run down.

*You look totally **busted**. You should have worn something nicer than ripped <u>sweats</u>.*

caked on (adj) ◯ If a woman's makeup is **caked on,** she is wearing way too much—so much that it looks like it has been applied to the face with a trowel.

*That girl's makeup is so **caked on** that I can see the line of her foundation from across the room!*

cap (n) ◯ A **cap** is a hat and usually refers specifically to a baseball hat.

*Students, please take off your **caps** when you are indoors in this class.*

capris (n) ◯ **Capris** are short pants that stop below the knee and above the ankles, usually worn by women and in warm weather.

*I can't wear **capris**. I'm so short that they fit me like full-length pants!*

cargo pants (n) ◯ **Cargo pants** are cotton, military-style pants with a large pocket on the outside of each leg in the knee area. **Cargo pants** have become very popular over the last few years, as have cargo shorts (which are the short version of the pants).

*I love **cargo pants** because I can hold so much stuff in the pockets; they're really convenient.*

cords (n) ◯ **Cords** are corduroy pants. These are very popular and stylish in many parts of the United States, especially in cold-weather climates, because **cords** are very warm.

*Sharon has eight pairs of **cords,** all in different colors. She says that's how she gets through the snowy school days.*

decked out (adj) ○ Someone who is <u>dressed up</u> is **decked out.** People usually get all **decked out** for events such as parties, <u>black-tie</u> affairs, and dates.

> *Woman 1: You're all **decked out.** Where are you going?*
>
> *Woman 2: Just to class, but I'm trying to look nice for this guy I have a <u>crush</u> on.*

diesel (adj) ○ **Diesel** means well developed in terms of muscles. So, a large bodybuilder is **diesel.**

> *I wouldn't mess with that guy. He's **diesel**, and he'll totally kick your butt!*

doo rag (n) ○ A **doo rag** is a bandanna worn on the head. This has become especially popular with girls on college campuses in the last few years.

> *I don't have time to wash my hair before class, so I'll just put on a **doo rag** and wear some <u>sweats</u>.*

dreds (n) ○ **Dreds** is an abbreviated slang term for dreadlocks, a hairstyle derived from the Rastafarian religion. Many college students have adopted **dreds,** if not the religion they represent.

> *Woman 1: Oh my! You shaved your head!*
>
> *Woman 2: Yes. I had **dreds** for years, and I had to shave them off to get rid of them.*

dress down (v, adj) ○ To **dress down** is to dress in casual clothes. This term can be used as an adjective; for example, a **dress-down** event is an event to which you can wear casual or weekend clothes.

> *This is a **dress-down** party, so why are you wearing <u>black-tie</u> attire?*

dressed to the nines (adj) ○ Someone who is **dressed to the nines** is dressed in fancy attire and looks very good.

*She was **dressed to the nines** for her date, but he never showed up. She got all dressed up for nothing.*

dress up (v) ○ This is the opposite of dress down. It means to dress more nicely than your everyday or casual wear.

*I have to **dress up** for my oral presentation to my law class, so I can't wear my favorite jeans!*

duds (n) ○ **Duds** are clothes. A synonym is **threads.**

*Woman 1: Hey, nice **duds.***
Woman 2: Thanks. I got this outfit yesterday.

fashionista (n) ○ A **fashionista** is a person who is very concerned with fashion and disapproves of anyone else whom she does not view as fashionable. A **fashionista** will be current with all the latest trends and may spend a lot of money on clothing.

*Being fashionable is one thing, but my roommate is such a **fashionista.** She hates the way everyone else dresses, and it takes her 2 hours every day to pick out something to wear!*

flippys (n) ○ **Flippys** is a shortened form of flip-flops. (See Chapter 1 for more information on flip-flops.)

*I hate **flippys,** even though they're so in right now. They hurt the space between my toes.*

fly (n) ○ Someone who is **fly** is cool or stylish. **Fly** can also mean attractive (or someone who is both stylish *and* attractive).

Those are some fly <u>kicks</u> you're wearing! They're the coolest sneakers I've seen.

full metal jacket (n) ○ **Full metal jacket** is slang for braces (the kind people wear to correct their teeth). Most people get braces when they are young, but some people in college do have braces. This term only applies to metal braces. Today, there are plastic and "invisible" braces as well.

   Man: Nice **full metal jacket.**

Woman: *That's mean! At least I'll have straight teeth when they're removed!*

funky (adj) ○ Something that is **funky** is off beat or unusual. People with their own sense of personal style that is outside the norm are often referred to as **funky.**

That's a really funky bracelet. I've never seen one like it before.

get-up (n) ○ A **get-up** is an outfit. This is usually used to describe a complicated and/or weird-looking outfit.

What kind of get-up is that? You look like an astronaut!

glam it up (n) ○ **Glam** is short for glamour, so to **glam it up** is to make yourself look glamorous. This term is usually used by and applied to women.

Althea really glammed it up for the <u>formal</u> on Friday night. She usually just wears jeans and T-shirts.

got it going on (n) ⟳ Someone who's **got it going on** is attractive and well dressed.

*That girl's really **got it going on**. I'm going to ask her for a date.*

Goth (n) ⟳ **Goth** is short for gothic and is a style of life and dress that is dramatic. People who are **Goth** commonly dress in all black, prefer pale skin and <u>funky</u> clothing, and often wear dark red or black lipstick.

*My <u>roommate</u> is a **Goth**. She wears all black all the time and black lipstick, and I'm a <u>preppy</u>, so we make quite a contrasting pair.*

hat head (n) ⟳ This refers to the flattening of the hair underneath a hat.

*I can't take off my hat because I've been wearing it all day. I have total **hat head!***

hippie (n) ⟳ A **hippie** is someone who is into nature and peace. The phrase was coined in the 1960s to describe people who protested the Vietnam War and sometimes lived on communes and took drugs. The definition is looser today—many people dress in earthy, **hippie**-type clothing but do not consider themselves **hippies** in the traditional sense. (Also see page 90)

*My <u>roommate</u> is a vegetarian and only listens to Phish. She's a total **hippie**.*

hoodie (n) ⟳ A **hoodie** is a hooded sweatshirt. **Hoodies** are very common on college campuses and can be either pullovers or zip-ups.

*Has anyone seen my **hoodie**? It's raining, and I need a hood.*

in (n) ⟳ Something that is **in** is fashionable at the moment.

*Tall boots are so **in** right now. Everyone is wearing them.*

kicks (n) ○ **Kicks** are shoes and sneakers.

> Woman 1: *Hey, nice **kicks**. May I borrow them?*
> Woman 2: *I don't know. What shoe size are you?*

lid (n) ○ A **lid** is any type of hat.

> *That's a great **lid**. It covers up your bad haircut!*

low-rise jeans (n) ○ These are jeans that sit on the waist below a person's belly button. These jeans have become popular in the last year or so.

> *Don't you get cold wearing those **low-rise jeans** in the winter?*

macked out (adj) ○ Someone who is **macked out** is dressed stylishly. A synonym is **pimped out.** This term can also describe something such as a house or car or <u>dorm</u> room that has lots of amenities.

> *He's all **macked out** for his date with some pretty girl.*

monkey suit (n) ○ A **monkey suit** is a tuxedo; also sometimes referred to as a **penguin suit.**

> *I have to wear a **monkey suit** to this <u>black-tie</u> affair tonight.*

mullet (n) ○ A **mullet** is a hairstyle consisting of short hair on the top and sides of the head, with long hair in the back, usually worn by men, but not exclusively.

> *That **mullet** is so last decade!*

off the hook (n) ○ Someone who looks so good that it's almost unbelievable looks **off the hook.** This can also describe an object that is really great.

*That car is **off the hook**—it has heated seats, a DVD player, and a built-in coffee maker!*

old school (adj) ○ **Old school** is similar to retro, but often refers to fashion from the early 1980s rap era.

*Those Adidas Sambas are so **old school.***

out (n) ○ **Out** means "out of style" or "not fashionable." (Also see page 31)

*That guy has a mullet! That's so **out** right now.*

preppy (adj, n) ○ **Preppy** clothing is classic clothing, simple and unadorned. This term is derived from the preparatory school-style of chinos, white shirt, and striped tie. When you think of **preppy**, think of tennis clothing, collared shirts, and well-tailored clothing. The noun form is **preppy** (or **preppie**), designating a person who dresses in this style.

*That guy is too **preppy** and conservative for me.*

put on a few (v) ○ To **put on a few** is to gain weight.

*I've **put on a few** because I've been drinking too much beer, which is so fattening.*

retro (adj) ○ **Retro** refers to styles, clothing, cars, and furniture that come from previous decades.

*That girl is so **retro**. Her outfit looks like something that came right out of the 1970s!*

six pack (n) ○ **Six pack** refers to visable abdominal muscles on a person who works out a lot.

*That guy has a great **six pack**. He must do sit-ups all day every day!*

slum around (v) ○ To **slum around** is to wear lounge clothes—usually old, comfortable, not-nice clothes—for the sake of comfort. On many college campuses, **slumming around** is the preferred style of dress. You may even see people in class wearing pajama bottoms and a sweatshirt!

*I was **slumming around** today. I ran out to the store wearing my grossest <u>sweats</u>, and, of course, ran into the guy I had a <u>crush</u> on.*

spacers (n) ○ **Spacers** are tubular jewelry worn in the ears in place of traditional earrings. **Spacers** eventually space out the ear hole, which does not stretch back. They can range from a tiny tube to a tube that's two inches in diameter (or even bigger).

*The guy who sits in front of me in art history has **spacers** in his ears that are so big I can see the art slides through them.*

specs (n) ○ **Specs** are eyeglasses or sunglasses.

*Has anyone seen my **specs**? I can't see anything without them.*

sport (v) ○ To **sport** something is to wear it.

*I'm **sporting** a glamorous look today.*

stylin' (n) ◯ Someone who is **stylin'** is highly fashionable and is wearing <u>cool</u> clothes. If you are even more stylish than **stylin'**, you're **superstylin'**.

> *Man 1: How do you like my new look?*
>
> *Man 2: You're **stylin'**, man. All the ladies will love you.*

sweats (n) ◯ **Sweats** are pants and shirts made of sweatshirt material, which is a warm and densely woven cotton weave. **Sweats** are worn for hanging out and for exercising—and to class when you're <u>slumming around</u>.

> *Nice **sweats**! You look so comfortable.*

tacky (adj) ◯ Something that is **tacky** is cheap looking or <u>cheesy</u>.

> *That blouse is so **tacky**. You have no <u>taste</u> in clothes.*

taste (n) ◯ As it relates to appearance, **taste** means preference. Some people have a **taste** in clothes that is conservative, for example, whereas other people's taste is more wild.

> *You have really good **taste** in clothes. I could never put together a killer outfit like that.*

tight (n) ◯ Someone who is **tight** is very good looking, or more specifically, someone who is a <u>hottie</u>.

> *You look **tight** today. Do you want to go get a drink later?*

Tims (n) ○ **Tims** is an abbreviated slang term for Timberland, a brand of hiking boots and outdoor shoes. For many people, **Tims** are simply a fashion statement, but for those who go to school in cold climates, shoes such as **Tims** are a necessity.

*I walked to class through five inches of snow, but my **Tims** kept my feet warm and dry.*

trendy (adj) ○ Someone who wears clothes that follow the latest trends is **trendy.** The opposite of **trendy** is **classic** (someone who wears classic clothes).

*That boy is so **trendy,** he changes his look every two weeks!*

unibrow (n) ○ A person who has thick eyebrows that touch in the middle has a **unibrow**—literally, *one brow.*

*That guy has a total **unibrow**. He should shave the middle.*

wraps (n) ○ **Wraps** are sunglasses.

*I can't find my **wraps,** and it's so sunny out!*

8

The Book of Love—Dating and Relationships

Let's face it, the college experience includes social stuff as well as academics. Looking for romance is a major college pastime. So, it's no surprise that a lot of college slang revolves around dating. In this chapter, you'll find words and phrases about love and relationships and, of course, dating.

all over (someone) (v) ○ To be **all over someone** is to display an obvious and possibly excessive affection for someone else through physical contact.

Adam is such a jerk! We went out on a date last night, and tonight he's been all over Jennifer!

betty (adj) ○ A **betty** is a pretty or desirable girl.

That girl is such a betty! I'm going to try to talk to her.

blind date (n) ○ A **blind date** is a date in which the two parties do not know one another before the date. **Blind dates** are often set up by mutual friends.

> Woman 1: *I know this guy who would be totally great for you. Do you want me to fix you up on a date?*
>
> Woman 2: *I don't know . . . I haven't had much luck with **blind dates**.*

booty call (n) ○ A **booty call** is a visit made to a friend for the purpose of intimate relations. This can also be the term used to describe the actual person with whom someone is having intimate relations. **Booty** is a slang term for someone's posterior.

> *Brad showed up at my door last night for a **booty call**, and we haven't even spoken for three weeks!*

boyfriend (n) ○ A **boyfriend** is a man with whom someone has an exclusive relationship.

> *Andrew is the best **boyfriend** I've ever had. I could really see myself marrying him.*

break (someone's) *heart* (v) ○ To **break someone's heart** is to end a relationship with someone who is in love with you.

> *Allie **broke my heart**. I don't know if I can ever trust myself to fall in love again after that.*

break up (v) ○ When two people end a romantic relationship, they **break up.**

> Woman 1: *Paige **broke up** with Jared.*
>
> Woman 2: *Why? I thought they were so happy together.*
>
> Woman 1: *She found out he was cheating on her.*

brush off (v, n) ↻ To disregard or not take seriously someone who is romantically interested in you is to **brush him or her off** (verb). When this happens, you have given that person the **brush off** (noun).

*That boy over there has been trying to talk to me all night. I already gave him the **brush off** like, an hour ago, but he just keeps trying!*

casual dating (n) ↻ Casual dating is when two people date each other, but not seriously, and often also date other people.

*I'm in support of **casual dating** because I don't want to be tied down to one person. There are just too many great people to meet in college!*

cheating (v) ↻ Having a romantic relationship with one person while dating a second person without the first person's knowledge is **cheating.** If you **cheat** on someone, you may break that person's heart.

*Jillian is **cheating** on me with some scrawny loser from her dorm.*

chick (n) ↻ **Chick** means "girl." This term is used widely, but some people consider it offensive, so use it with care!

*Aviva is the cutest **chick** in this dorm. I wonder if she has a boyfriend already.*

chickenhead (n) ↻ This is a term that describes a woman who has intimate relations with many men or acts with loose morals. This is not a nice thing to call someone!

*Ugh! That girl is such a **chickenhead**! Last week she hooked up with my roommate, and today she tried to get with me!*

crush (n) ◯ If you have an infatuation with someone, you have a **crush** on that person.

*I have a huge **crush** on this boy in my bio class . . . he is so cute!*

cutie (n) ◯ A **cutie** is an attractive, or cute, person. This term usually applies to men.

*Jay is such a **cutie** that I just want to pinch his cheeks every time I see him!*

digits (n) ◯ **Digits** means "phone number." So, if someone asks for your **digits,** that person is asking for your phone number.

   *Man: You're cute. May I get your **digits**?*

Woman: No way! I don't give out my number to strangers!

double date (n) ◯ A **double date** is a date in which two couples go out together.

*My roommate and I are going on a **double date** with the two girls who live next door.*

dumped (v) ◯ If someone ceases a romantic relationship with you, you have been **dumped.**

*Mark **dumped** me for some chickenhead he met at a party last week.*

ex (n) ◯ People refer to former boyfriends and girlfriends as **ex's,** which is an abbreviation of ex-girlfriend or ex-boyfriend.

*I wouldn't date that girl if I were you; she still has feelings for her **ex**.*

eye candy (n) ↺ This is a term usually applied to women, and it means attractive or nice to look at.

*His new <u>girlfriend</u> is such **eye candy,** I could look at her all day!*

fall for (someone) (v) ↺ To **fall for** someone is to begin to develop romantic feelings for that person. You can also **fall** in love.

*We've been dating for a couple of months now, and I think I'm **falling for** you.*

fifth wheel (n) ↺ When several couples go out and one single person joins them, the single person is the **fifth wheel**. (A car has four wheels, so the fifth wheel denotes an extra wheel [person].) The number of people in the group does not matter; the extra person is always the fifth wheel.

*My <u>roommate's boyfriend</u> is visiting, and I just feel like a **fifth wheel** when I hang out with them; I know they'd rather be alone.*

fix someone up (v) ↺ To **fix someone up** with another person is to make the arrangements for these two people to get together for a date. Also see <u>blind date</u>.

*That guy Gary in my communications class would be perfect for my friend Donna. I'll have to **fix them up.***

fling (n) ↺ A **fling** is a brief romantic relationship.

Woman 1: Who's that boy that you were talking to?

*Woman 2: Some guy I had a **fling** with on <u>spring break</u>. He just transferred here.*

friends with privilege (n) ◯ **Friends with privileges** are two people who are friends who occasionally have intimate relations (privileges).

I don't have a <u>boyfriend</u> *right now, but I have Brad, who's a **friend with privileges**. But if I find a guy to date, no more "privileges" for Brad.*

game (n) ◯ Someone who has **game** is very good at meeting new romantic interests. Someone who has no **game** has no luck in the romantic arena.

*You've got no **game**, dude. That girl will never* <u>go out</u> *with you!*

get the green light (v) ◯ To **get the green light** is to get permission from someone to initiate intimate relations.

*Jane finally **gave me the green light** to kiss her goodnight, which I'm really happy about, because it's our fifth date!*

get with (v) ◯ To **get with** someone is to either get acquainted with that person or have intimate relations with him or her.

*I've got to **get with** that boy; he's such a* <u>hottie</u>.

girlfriend (n) ◯ A **girlfriend** is a woman with whom someone has an exclusive relationship.

I can't <u>go out</u> *with you, I already have a **girlfriend**.*

go out (v) ◯ This means to go on a date with someone or to be dating one person exclusively.

*Sara has been **going out** with Tomas for several weeks now. They make a cute couple.*

going Dutch (v) ↻ When two people go on a date and each of them pays for half of the expenses on the date, they are **going Dutch.**

> *Angel and I went to dinner last night, and he wanted to **go Dutch**! He asked me out on the date, so I really think he should have paid.*

going steady (v) ↻ Two people who have an exclusive romantic relationship are said to be **going steady.** This is a somewhat dated term, but you'll encounter it from time to time, especially if you watch old movies.

> *Aaron and Alexis have been **going steady** for three years. I'm sure they'll get married after graduation.*

hook up (v) ↻ To **hook up** is to engage in intimate relations with someone. You will find this term to be quite common on campus.

> *Chris **hooked up** with Jamal's <u>girlfriend</u>, and now Jamal won't speak to Chris!*

hottie (n) ↻ A **hottie** is an attractive and desirable person. Some synonyms are **knockout, stud,** and **fox.**

> *That guy is such a **hottie**! He's the best looking boy on campus.*

lady killer (n) ↻ A man who dates a lot of women or is very successful with women is a **lady killer.**

> *Amos thinks he's such a **lady killer**! He dates a different girl every weekend!*

mack on (v) ↻ To **mack on** someone is to ask that person for a date or to try to get that person to like you romantically.

*I'm totally **macking on** that <u>hottie</u> over there; I'm going to see if he wants to dance.*

on the outs (v) ↻ When two people in a relationship are fighting or not speaking to one another, they are **on the outs.** This term usually implies that the couple will get back together.

*Woman 1: Morris and Emily are **on the outs,** so you should ask him out.*
Woman 2: No way, they'll be back together by the weekend.

on the rebound (v) ↻ Someone who is **on the rebound** has just ended a relationship. Common "wisdom" says one shouldn't date someone who is **on the rebound,** because rebound relationships have a high rate of failure.

*Sarah's totally **on the rebound** from her breakup with Kevin, so don't get too involved with her and become her "rebound relationship."*

one-night stand (n) ↻ A **one-night stand** is when two people have sexual intercourse just one time, and never get together again any time after the fact. This denotes a "meaningless" sexual encounter.

*I had a **one-night stand** last night, and I feel horrible; the walk home was a total <u>walk of shame</u>.*

other fish in the sea (n) ☊ When someone is <u>dumped</u>, people often offer the advice "there are **other fish in the sea,**" which means that there are plenty of other people in the world with whom someone can have a relationship.

*Don't worry, Ariana, there are **other fish in the sea,** and you'll find someone else way better than Danny.*

PDA (n) ☊ This stands for Public Displays of Affection, which is pretty self-explanatory. Holding hands and kissing or being <u>all over someone</u> are **PDAs.**

*I hate **PDAs**! I wish people would keep their affection to themselves and behave in public.*

pickup lines (n) ☊ **Pickup lines** are phrases used by people to open up a conversation with someone to whom they are attracted. **Pickup lines** denote trite, overused lines, and they should be used with care . . . or not at all. Simply saying hello to someone is a better way to strike up a conversation than using some <u>cheesy</u> line.

> Man: *Hey, baby. Your father must have taken the stars from the skies and put them in your eyes!*
>
> Woman: *That is the worst **pickup line** I've ever heard! Go away!*

player (n) ☊ A **player** is a person who dates many people at the same time with no regard to the feelings of the people he or she is dating.

*Don't even speak to that guy, he's a total **player**. He was dating both of my <u>roommates</u> at the same time.*

put out (v) ⊃ To **put out** is to allow someone to have intimate relations with you.

*I won't **put out** until I'm married.*

put the moves on (v) ⊃ To **put the moves on** someone is to try to initiate intimate relations with that person.

*That creep **put the moves on** me, and we just met!*

seeing someone (v) ⊃ If you are **seeing someone,** you are dating that person, but not necessarily exclusively.

    *Man: Is your friend **seeing anyone**?*

Woman: No, why don't you ask her to go out on a date with you?

sleep with (v) ⊃ To **sleep with** someone is to have intercourse with that person. This is probably one of the most common, nonvulgar terms for intercourse.

*Did you **sleep with** him?*

slutty (adj) ⊃ This is a term that usually refers to women of loose sexual morals, although recently, it has begun to be used to refer to men as well.

*That boy is so **slutty**! He hooks up all the time.*

stalker (n) ○ A **stalker** is someone who has an obsession with a person that may manifest itself in a dangerous and violent way. If you think someone is stalking you in this way, get help from the police. However, this term is commonly used in a joking manner.

*This is the third time I've seen you today! Are you a **stalker** or something?*

sugar daddy (n) ○ A **sugar daddy** is a man who showers his romantic interest with gifts. A woman who does the same would be a **sugar mama.**

Woman 1: How does she afford all that <u>cool</u> stuff?
*Woman 2: She's dating some **sugar daddy**. He buys her all kinds of gifts.*

swept off my feet (v) ○ To be **swept off your feet** is to have someone impress you greatly in a romantic way.

*My date gave me a dozen roses and arranged for a private meal in a posh restaurant . . . he really **swept me off my feet**. I think I'm in love!*

totally into (v) ○ When you really like someone romantically, you are **totally into** that person. You can also be **totally into** things such as music, studying, surfing, and so on.

*I'm **totally into** that guy because I love skiing and he's **totally into** skiing, too!*

turn off (n) ○ Something that is a **turn off** is sexually unappealing. In common use, this can be applied to anything that is unappetizing.

*Overconfident people are such a **turn off** to me.*

walk of shame (n) ◯ The walk home after a <u>one-night stand</u> is the **walk of shame.**

> *I walked a mile to get home this morning from this guy's house; it was a long **walk of shame**—I'll never put myself in that position again.*

yeti (n) ◯ A **yeti** is a mythologic creature that is said to be an unnaturally huge, hair-covered being or monster that lives in the mountains. **Yeti** is also a slang term for a really unattractive person. This is a very cruel thing to call someone.

> *She's a **yeti**. You're way too attractive for her.*

9

Having Fun—Music and Leisure

College life is half study and half leisure activities. We've covered some leisure activities, such as dating and partying, in individual chapters. In this chapter, you'll find words about music, cars and driving, games, and other assorted activities.

air hockey (n) ○ **Air hockey** is a table hockey game in which the table is perforated with tiny holes through which air flows, allowing the plastic puck to move across the table. **Air hockey** is played by two people at a time.

*I beat Jennie in **air hockey** three times this week. I'm so glad we have the table in the <u>lounge</u>.*

alternative (n) ○ **Alternative** is a kind of music that is outside of the <u>mainstream</u>, <u>Top 40</u> list. However, over the years, bands like Nirvana and Pearl Jam, part of the "Seattle sound" or "<u>grunge</u>" movement, have retained the style of **alternative** music while also becoming mainstream.

   Man: What bands do you like?
*Woman: I listen to **alternative**.*

back-seat driver (n) ◌ The literal meaning of **back-seat driver** is someone who gives directions to the driver from the back seat of a car (which still holds true). In common use, **back-seat driver** describes any person who gives unwanted and unsolicited advice to another person.

Woman 1: You should really study with flashcards.

*Woman 2: Stop being such a **back-seat driver**. I know how to study!*

BBQ (n) ◌ BBQ is <u>short for</u> barbecue, which is the cooking of food on an outdoor grill. Socially, people often gather for **BBQs** in the summer or warmer months, unless they live in a warmer climate all year long. We've included it here instead of the food chapter  because although the act of barbecuing itself is not a social event, having a **BBQ** is.

*We're having a really big **BBQ** this Saturday. We have enough <u>hot dogs</u> and hamburgers for fifty people!*

Beemer (n) ◌ This is a slang term for the car brand BMW.

*My <u>boyfriend</u> drives a **Beemer**.*

boob tube (n) ◌ Also known as the **idiot box,** a **boob tube** is a television. **Tube** itself is a slang term for television. Some people feel that watching TV is an activity that makes people unintelligent, thus, **boob tube.**

*You are such a <u>couch potato</u>. All you do is sit and watch the **boob tube** all day!*

boy band (n) ○ **Boy band** is a term for a band composed of boys who sing and do not play instruments. This term also implies that the band is manufactured, that is, the members were put together by a third party and did not form the band themselves.

*'N Sync is a **boy band**.*

boys'/girls' night out (n) ○ **Boys' night out** is a night when a group of men go out without women. This term implies that the men are all in relationships, and **boys' night out** is their night to <u>hang out</u> with their male friends. **Girls' night out** means the same thing but, of course, the people going out are women.

*Thursday is **boys' night out** because Scott's <u>girlfriend</u> won't let him party with us on a weekend night.*

bumper sticker (n) ○ A **bumper sticker** is a sticker that is placed on the bumper or the back window of a car that represents or has a slogan that represents something of importance to the driver.

*I got a **bumper sticker** that says "Save the Whales."*

catch a show (v) ○ To **catch a show** is to go see a movie at the movie theater.

*Do you want to **catch a show** after dinner tonight? We can see that new movie.*

catch some rays (v) ○ To **catch some rays** is to lay in the sun with the purpose of getting a tan.

*I'm going to go outside in my bathing suit and try to **catch some rays** before it gets too cloudy.*

celeb (n) ↻ **Celeb** is a slang abbreviation of "celebrity." Celebrities are famous people, and you will often hear them referred to as **celebs** on TV and in magazines. Few people call them **celebs** in common conversation.

This month's issue of Famous People Magazine *has an article on one of my favorite* ***celebs*** *this week.*

chick flick (n) ↻ A **flick** is a movie. A **chick flick** is a movie whose target audience is women. This is a stereotypical statement; nonetheless, you're bound to hear it.

I'm going to the movies with my girlfriend, *and she's going to make me see some stupid* ***chick flick*** *when I'd rather see that movie about baseball.*

chillin' out (v) ↻ **Chillin' out** is to be with your friend(s) or by yourself and relax. **Chillin' out** is a major college pastime! You may find yourself **chillin' out** with friends often.

Charlie and I just ***chilled out*** *last night and watched TV. We were too tired to do anything else, but it was fun.*

clambake (n) ↻ A **clambake** is a party on the beach at which there is usually a barbecue of seafood and, of course, clams.

We had a ***clambake*** *last night, and then we fell asleep on the beach.*

classic rock (n) ↻ **Classic rock** denotes any type of music from the late 1960s to the early 1980s.

The Beatles are ***classic rock***.

clubbing (v) ◯ **Clubbing** is the act of going out to different dance clubs during a night.

*We went **clubbing** until 3 a.m. this morning!*

clunker (n) ◯ A **clunker** is an old, falling-apart car.

*My old **clunker** broke down three times last week, and today it won't start.*

cruise (v) ◯ To **cruise** is to drive around in your car. **Cruising** is a popular pastime in some places, where cars usually drive up and down a main road. In other uses, a person can **cruise** to look for something, as in "I'm going to **cruise** around the store until I find what I want."

*We got a traffic ticket Saturday night for **cruising**. You can only drive down the main street twice an hour, and we drove around four times.*

Deadhead (n) ◯ A **Deadhead** is a fan of the band named The Grateful Dead.

*My brother is such a **Deadhead**. In the 1980s, he went <u>on tour</u> with The Grateful Dead for an entire year!*

down the shore (n) ◯ **Down the shore** means "at the beach." This is a regional expression generally heard in the Philadelphia, Pennsylvania, area and New Jersey.

*Let's go **down the shore** this weekend and do some surfing.*

drag race (n) ◯ A **drag race** (in nonprofessional race-driving terms) is an illegal race between two people either in an open space or on public streets. This type of **drag racing** is dangerous.

*Her brother got into an accident while **drag racing** and lost his driver's license for a year!*

drop someone off (v) ☉ This is a driving-related term. To **drop someone off** is to drive a person to a designated place.

*Let's go for dessert, and then I'll **drop you off** at your <u>dorm</u>.*

fender bender (n) ☉ A **fender bender** is a minor automobile accident.

*I got into a **fender bender** in the snow. I hit the back of the car in front of me.*

folk music (n) ☉ **Folk music** contains a social message in the lyrics and is often played on acoustic instruments. The 1960s saw a surge in folk music.

*I wrote a **folk song** for my music class about the plight of the Canadian geese in New Jersey.*

fooseball (n) ☉ **Fooseball** is a table game of soccer composed of wooden players on sticks. Up to six people can play a game of **fooseball** at once.

*My <u>boyfriend</u> won his fraternity's **fooseball** tournament.*

freestyle (n) ☉ **Freestyle** is a "game" of rap in which two rappers face off in a contest.

The movie 8 Mile *with Eminem was about **freestyle** rap.*

Frisbee golf (n) ☉ A **Frisbee** is a plastic disc thrown between two or more people in a game of catch. In **Frisbee golf**, players have to throw the Frisbee toward designated areas, similar to holes in golf, to gather points. This game has become very popular on some campuses.

*I am the **Frisbee golf** champion of my <u>dorm</u>!*

groove (v) ◯ To **groove** is to dance. **Groove** can also mean a musical beat.

Groove to the music.

grunge (n) ◯ This is a form of <u>alternative</u> music made popular by several bands out of the Seattle, Washington, area, such as Pearl Jam and Alice in Chains. A little heavy and dark, **grunge** became more than just music, it also became a style. **Grunge** musicians wore a "uniform" of ripped jeans and thermal T-shirts with flannel shirts over that, and this style became popular with youth nationwide. **Grunge** changed the face of <u>Top 40</u> music for a while, from light pop tunes to the more heavy songs.

*You should tell your <u>roommate</u> that the **grunge** look went out of style in 1994!*

hang a (left, right) (v) ◯ In a car (or even when walking), if someone says "**hang a left**," it means "turn to the left." By the same token, **hang a right** means "go to the right." Also see <u>louie</u> and <u>ralph</u>.

*Go to the bookstore and **hang a right** at the next corner. Then walk for two blocks and you'll find the Science Building.*

hang out (v) ◯ To **hang out** is one of the most popular activities on college campuses. **Hanging out** means spending time with your friends, usually watching TV and having conversation. **Hang out** can also generically mean "spend time with." So, if you are **hanging out** tonight with a friend, you are spending time tonight with that friend.

*I just want to **hang out** tonight. I'm too tired to go out.*

heavy metal (n) ◯ This is a type of music made popular in the 1980s that consists of loud, piercing guitar music with fast melodies. Many **heavy metal** bands, such as Metallica and Motley Crüe, had members who looked like tough guys with long hair. This form of music has survived through the 1990s and into this century with new bands such as Linkin Park and Rage Against the Machine.

*I love **heavy metal,** and I don't like* <u>rap</u> *music.*

hip-hop (n) ◯ **Hip-hop** is a form of <u>rap</u> music.

*I'm a big fan of **hip-hop** music.*

hit the road (v) ◯ **Hit the road** is a driving term. It means "to leave in a car."

*Let's **hit the road** before the snow gets too deep. My car has really bad traction in the snow.*

jam bands (n) ◯ **Jam bands** are bands that don't play a predetermined set list at concerts and usually play free-form jams in songs. The Grateful Dead was the most popular jam band, having invented the free-form set-list format. **Jam bands** today, such as Phish and Moe, model their live performance style on The Grateful Dead's performance style.

*I'm really into **jam bands,** so it's weird to me to see a concert where there is no musical jamming.*

karaoke (n) ◯ **Karaoke** is a machine that provides background music and lyrics to popular songs so a person with a microphone can sing along with the music. **Karaoke** has become quite popular in the past decade, and you will find that many bars have **karaoke** nights where you can pay a small fee (if it's not free) to sing with the machine in front of all the bar patrons.

*Did you hear Jen do **karaoke** at the bar last night? She has the worst singing voice I've ever heard!*

lay out (v) ◯ To **lay out** is to lie on a chair or blanket in the sun for the purpose of getting a tan. On a sunny warm day in college, you may see people **laying out** on grassy areas. See also catch some rays.

*I **laid out** yesterday because it was so warm, and I got a sunburn!*

louie (n) ◯ A **louie** is a left turn. This term is usually used when driving or giving someone else driving directions.

*Hang a **louie** at the next traffic light.*

mainstream (n) ◯ **Mainstream** is music that is on the Billboard Top 40 list of popular songs. **Mainstream music** appeals to a mass amount of people and is often referred to as **pop music.**

*I listen to **mainstream** music, because I don't like rap or alternative.*

mini-golf (n) ◯ This is an abbreviated slang term for miniature golf, which is a recreational, family game played with putters. **Mini-golf** is a popular game, especially in coastal and beach towns.

*I am the **mini-golf** champion of my sorority. We have a tournament every year, and I've won the past two years!*

on tour (v) ○ This phrase has two meanings. When a musical band is **on tour,** it means the band is traveling from city to city performing concerts. A second meaning of **on tour** is associated with jam bands, where fans of certain jam bands follow the band while the band is on tour to see all of the shows the band performs.

*I went **on tour** with Phish one summer, and I saw thirty shows and traveled all across the country!*

Phish head (n) ○ A **Phish head** is a fan of the band Phish, which is one of the most well-known and successful jam bands in the United States.

*My roommate is a total **Phish head**! She's seen the band more than 100 times!*

pool (n) ○ Also known as **billiards,** pool is a table game in which people use sticks called *cues* to hit balls into certain pockets on a table. This is a very popular game in bars, and there are also places called **pool halls** that consist of many **pool** tables on which people can play.

*I don't like to play **pool**. My aim is not good.*

pop (n) ○ **Pop** is a slang abbreviation for popular music. **Pop** music is usually melodic and has mass appeal. Britney Spears is an example of a **pop** artist. However, **pop** music is always changing, because it is based on what is popular with the majority of the public at a certain time. (Also see page 60)

***Pop** music is too lighthearted for me. I prefer heavy metal.*

punk (n) ○ **Punk** is a type of music that is loud and heavy, yet its basic melody is based on old time, 1950s-era rock and roll. Some popular **punk** bands are Blink 182 and Sum 41. Bands such as The Ramones and The Sex Pistols helped to create **punk** in the 1970s, and today's **punk** bands base their music on the music of these founders.

*I love **punk** music because the melodies and lyrics are loud and catchy.*

R&B (n) ○ **R&B** is an abbreviation of Rhythm and Blues, which is a type of music based on jazz and rock and roll. Some popular **R&B** artists are Ashanti and Destiny's Child.

R&B is so soothing to listen to.

ralph (n) ○ **Ralph** is the opposite of louie. It means "right" and is usually used while driving or giving directions and is usually preceded by the phrase "hang a . . . ."

*Hang a **ralph** at the second stop sign, and you'll see my house on the left.*

rap (n) ○ **Rap** is music in which the lyrics are spoken in a rhythm rather than sung. Some examples of **rap** artists are Run-D.M.C., Eminem, and Nelly.

*I love **rap** music, but rapping is so hard to do because I have no rhythm.*

reggae (n) ○ **Reggae** music originated in Jamaica, mostly out of the Rastafarian religion, and it was made popular worldwide by Bob Marley.

*When I hear **reggae,** it makes me think of warm tropical places.*

ride (n) ○ Your **ride** is your car. A sweet **ride** is a really nice car. A synonym is **wheels.**

Do you want to see my new **ride***? It's a Porsche!*

rims (n) ○ **Rims** are the fancy hubcaps inside of tires. Because automobiles are a huge pastime in America, many people "dress up" their cars with extras, such as fancy **rims**.

Nice **rims***! They look a lot better than the standard ones that come with the car. Were they expensive?*

road trip (n) ○ A **road trip** is a popular leisure activity for some college students. A **road trip** includes a group of friends traveling somewhere far in a car. Sometimes, the **road trip** can be as much fun as the final destination. This is a popular way to travel in America due to the national Interstate System, which makes travel across the country very easy (except for the distance).

My best friends and I drove to Florida from Delaware for spring break. It took us three days, and the car broke down four times, but we had so much fun that it was the best **road trip** *ever!*

rocking (adj) ○ **Rocking** means really good, usually used in reference to concerts or parties. The term comes from the **rock** in rock and roll.

That concert was **rocking***! The band sounded amazing!*

shotgun (n) ○ **Shotgun** is the position in the passenger seat of a car. When a group of people is heading somewhere in a car, the first person to yell "shotgun!" gets to sit up front with the driver.

Woman 1: Shotgun!

Woman 2: No fair! You got to sit in the front yesterday!

Woman 1: Tough, I called it first!

spin (v) ○ To **spin** is to act as a disc jockey and play records.

My girlfriend is spinning at the dance club tonight. She's its first woman disc jockey.

surfing the Web (v) ○ **Surfing the Web** means looking on the World Wide Web for interesting things as a form of entertainment.

I surfed the Web for 5 hours last night, and now my hand hurts from clicking the mouse so much!

system (n) ○ When referring to automobiles, **system** refers to the sound (or music) system, including the speakers.

I had a custom system built into my car, and you can hear the music from miles away when I play it.

techno (n) ○ **Techno** is loud, pulsating music meant to be danced to that consists of beats from records or synthesizers, as opposed to traditional instruments. Many dance clubs play **techno** music. Moby is an example of a **techno** musician.

I don't like techno. I prefer punk.

Top 40 (n) ○ **Top 40** refers to the list of songs compiled by *Billboard Magazine*, of the forty most popular songs played on <u>mainstream</u> stations throughout the country. *Billboard* keeps separate lists of popular songs for other genres of music, such as country music.

*If you have a song in the **Top 40** list for a long time, you are guaranteed to make a lot of money off the song.*

totaled (n) ○ After a car accident, if a car is damaged beyond repair, it is said to be **totaled.**

*My car was **totaled** in that accident last week, and now I have to get a new one!*

10

The Sporting Life—Sports Lingo

Whether playing sports, watching sports on TV, or attending sporting events, people in the United States love sports. Sports are so pervasive in American life that many slang expressions that are either about sports or derive from sports have entered the English language over the years. In this chapter, you'll find words and phrases that are sports specific or derive from sports, many of which have become common to use in nonsports-related situations.

Please note: We're not going to explain the rules of games such as baseball and football here; we're just going to define terms that are sports specific or terms that are derived from sports. For more information on the rules of various American sports, visit the following Web sites: www.nfl.com (football); www.mlb.com (baseball); www.nba.com (basketball); www.wnba.com (women's basketball); and www.espn.com (all types of sports).

ballpark figure (n) ○ A **ballpark figure** is a rough numeric estimate. This expression derives from something being "in the ballpark." The *ballpark* is the baseball field, and any hit within the park is **in the ballpark,** which has come to mean (in nonsports usage) "in the general area." So, "in the general area" translates into "an estimate," resulting in a **ballpark figure.**

I don't know exactly how many people will attend <u>homecoming</u> *celebrations this year, but I can give you a* ***ballpark figure.***

bandwagon (n) ○ In a sports context, on the **bandwagon** is to be in support of or a fan of a team. People are often said to jump on the **bandwagon,** which in the sports world means people who become fans of a team because that team is successful and popular with others.

I have been a fan of the Rocky Island Beavers team for twenty years, when they were a very bad team and almost no one came to games. Now that they're a successful team, so many people have jumped on the ***bandwagon*** *that the games are sold out!*

b-ball (n) ○ **B-ball** is an abbreviation of basketball.

Hey, do you want to play some ***b-ball****? The court's free for the next hour.*

belly flop (n) ○ In diving, if a diver does not go into the water headfirst, but instead lands in a horizontal position on his or her stomach (or *belly*), it is a **belly flop.** In common use, **belly flop** is used to mean "a mistake," usually a mistake made publicly.

My oral report in women's studies was a complete ***belly flop****! I couldn't remember any of my speech, and my visual aids didn't work!*

benched (v) ○ When a player on a team does something that causes the coach to not let him or her play, that player is **benched.** Being **benched** is not a good thing. However, some players play backup for starting positions, and these players are **bench** players, which is not a bad thing.

*Kevin used bad language in practice yesterday, so the coach **benched** him for the big game this weekend! Now we'll lose for sure—he's our best player.*

bleachers (n) ○ **Bleachers** are tiers of seats for spectators to sit on in athletic arenas or stadiums. They are usually made of metal or wood.

*The basketball game went into <u>overtime</u>. The people were so excited and jumping up and down that I thought the **bleachers** were going to collapse!*

bookie (n) ○ A **bookie** is someone who takes illegal sports bets. Betting on sports is illegal everywhere in the United States except for Las Vegas, Nevada, and at official horse-racing OTB (off-track betting) facilities.

*I lost a huge bet on a football game, and now I owe my **bookie** $500!*

brick (adj) ○ A basketball shot that misses the hoop and is not a good shot to begin with is called a **brick**.

*Jeremy had a chance for a game-winning shot . . . and he <u>choked</u>! His shot at the hoop was a **brick**— it hit the rim and bounced <u>out of bounds</u>!*

built like a linebacker (adj) ○ A **linebacker** is a defensive player in football. Linebackers are usually very large people, so if you say someone is **built like a linebacker,** you are saying that person is very large, but not necessarily overweight.

*I wouldn't get into a fight with that girl if I were you . . . she's **built like a linebacker,** and she'll totally destroy you!*

call the shots (v) ○ If you **call the shots**, you are solely in charge of something or in control of a situation. This phrase originated with target shooting, in which the shooter would announce, or call, where his or her shot would land, or another person would tell the shooter where to hit.

*Erin picked the ugliest dress for me to wear at her wedding. I hate it, but it's her wedding, so she's **calling the shots.***

choke (v) ○ When an athlete does not perform well in a high-pressure situation, it is said that he or she **choked.**

*Byron had the basketball with 3 seconds left in the game with a chance to score the winning shot, but he **choked** and threw a <u>brick</u>.*

die hard fan (n) ○ This is a <u>fan</u> who is extremely supportive of a sports team. A **die hard fan** is the kind of person who will camp out in a tent all night in front of the ticket office to get tickets to a game, or who will paint his or her face when attending a game.

*The Cameron Crazies at Duke University are **die hard fans.** They wait in line all night sometimes for tickets, and they are very rowdy at the games.*

fair play (adv) ○ **Fair play** is the act of abiding by the rules in sports and games. Outside of sports, a person plays fair when he or she shows fairness and honor in dealing with others.

*Show me some **fair play**. If I help you with your humanities report, you'll have to help me with my ancient civilizations report.*

fan (n) ◯ **Fan** is short for fanatic, and a **fan** is someone who likes and supports a certain team. Many people are fans of one team in each major sport. For example, someone may have a favorite baseball team, a favorite <u>football</u> team, and a favorite hockey team.

*I'm a **fan** of the New York Jets.*

field questions (v) ◯ This term comes from baseball, in which defensive players "field" the ball if it is hit to them. When people are making themselves available to answer questions from a crowd (or class, for instance), they **field questions.**

*I will lecture on the topic of Civil War medicine for the next 40 minutes, and then I will **field questions** about the lecture for an additional 20 minutes.*

football (n) ◯ What Europeans call **football,** Americans call *soccer*. In America, **football** is a sport that is derived from soccer, but in American football, players use their hands, as the ball is carried or passed. Football players don't touch the ball with their feet; there is a specialized position called *kicker,* whose job is to kick the ball if necessary (the ball is only kicked to score or to turn over possession). Football is a full-contact sport, which means that bodily contact is a part of the game.

*The San Diego Chiefs are a professional **football** team.*

fumble (v) ◯ This term derives from <u>football</u>. When a <u>football</u> player loses possession of the ball by dropping it before the play is done, it is called a **fumble.** This term can be used to describe anything someone does that is a mistake.

*Jane really **fumbled** on the oral exam in Spanish; she started speaking French!*

game plan (n) ◯ Every sport has a **game plan,** or a plan for how to play and win the game. This is an often-used term, and you'll hear it applied to all sorts of situations, from study plans to social plans.

> Woman 1: *There are four really good parties tonight, and we need to <u>hit</u> them all. So, what's the **game plan**?*
>
> Woman 2: *Well, we'll go to Jen's party first, and then we'll move on to Adam's house, and we'll decide from there about the other two parties.*

got game (v) ◯ In the sports world, **got game** refers to someone who is a talented athlete. However, you may hear this term used to describe someone who is <u>cool</u> or someone who is good at other things besides sports, such as dating, for instance.

> Man 1: *How did a <u>loser</u> like you get a date with that girl?*
>
> Man 2: *What can I say? I've **got game**.*

grand slam (n) ◯ A **grand slam** is when a baseball player hits a <u>home run</u> with a man on every base (a man in every possible scoring position). When used to refer to something outside of baseball, a **grand slam** means a "really good thing" or "a really successful endeavor."

> Woman: *How do you think my presentation in class went today?*
>
> Man: *You hit a **grand slam**. You're sure to get an A!*

gridiron (n) ◯ The **gridiron** is a <u>football</u> field, but can also refer to <u>football</u> in general. <u>Football</u> fields are marked by white lines at 5-yard intervals, thus turning the field into a grid.

> *Fall is **gridiron** season; I can't wait for the <u>football</u> games to start!*

home run (n) ○ A **home run** is a play in baseball in which the hitter hits the ball out of the park. Calling something not sports related a **home run** indicates a good outcome.

> *I really hit a **home run** at karaoke night. I won a $250 first prize in a contest!*

home stretch (n) ○ In baseball, the **home stretch** is the base-running area between third base and home plate (home plate is where a player can score). When a person is in the **home stretch** of something, he or she is almost finished.

> Woman: *I have to write a 40-page paper for my history class. I've been writing for three weeks, and I have five pages left to write.*
>
> Man: *Well, at least you're in the **home stretch**. You'll be finished soon!*

hoops (n) ○ **Hoops** is a slang term for basketball. Someone who plays basketball is a **hooper.**

> Man: *Are you going to the **hoops** game tonight?*
> Woman: *No, I don't like basketball.*

jock (n) ○ A **jock** is an athlete.

> *I really hope I have fun on my date with Joe; we're meeting after his football game. I don't usually date **jocks,** but I like Joe.*

March madness (n) ○ Division I NCAA basketball has a tournament every year in March that determines the champion. This time is called **March madness** and is a great time of year for college basketball fans.

> ***March madness** is such an exciting time in college basketball! I just love the tournament!*

nosebleed seats (n) ○ The **nosebleed seats** are the highest up (farthest away from the court or field) in a stadium or arena, so called because people can get nosebleeds at high altitudes. However, the altitude of the highest seat in any stadium will not give you a nosebleed, so this is a joking expression.

> Man: *Did you see that great play the quarterback made?*
>
> Woman: *No, I was sitting in the **nosebleed seats**, and I was too far away to see the play!*

no-win situation (n) ○ A **no-win situation** is a tie. When people are in **no-win situations,** they are in situations where they have no options that allow them to win.

> *I hate my professor and she hates me, so I'm in a **no-win situation**.*

on the ball (v) ○ To be **on the ball** is to be paying attention. This derives from baseball; a pitcher who is not having a good game and is not controlling the ball is said to be "off the ball," the opposite of which is **on the ball.**

> *If you were more **on the ball,** you wouldn't have forgotten that we have a paper due in class today!*

out of bounds (v) ○ Each sport has a playing field, and anything outside the field of play is **out of bounds.** In common usage, **out of bounds** can mean something that is outside of normal or something that crosses the boundaries of polite society or conversation.

> *You shouldn't have told Evan that he is a loser! That's really **out of bounds**.*

out of the park (adv) ○ In baseball, a ball that is hit out of the park in fair territory is a <u>home run</u>. A <u>home run</u> is a good thing, so if someone says you hit something **out of the park**, that person means that you did a good job.

*Wow! Your presentation on Abraham Lincoln was great! You really hit it **out of the park!** You'll get an A for sure!*

overtime (n) ○ **Overtime** is an extra time period added to a game to break a tie.

*The basketball game went into triple **overtime** before the home team finally won the game.*

packed house (n) ○ When a sports stadium or arena is completely full for an event, it is said to be a **packed house.**

*Joe Willie Stadium was filled to capacity for the first time last night, and the players really enjoyed playing for a **packed house.***

par for the course (n) ○ This term is derived from the sport of golf. **Par** on a golf course is the number of shots it should take you to complete a particular hole. If you play **par for the course** in golf, you've played a pretty good game, and it means you played the suggested average on every hole. In common use, **par for the course** means something that is ordinary or not suprising.

*Registering for classes was really not fun this year, but that's **par for the course,** because registration is never fun.*

pickup game (n) ○ A **pickup game** is a game, usually basketball, in which players who have just met play an unplanned game.

*I was so bored yesterday, that I went down to the park to see if I could join a **pickup game** or something. I joined a game, and the guys who I was playing with decided to start a basketball league, and they asked me to join.*

pigskin (n) ○ A **pigskin** is a football. Footballs used to be made of pigskin, but are now leather or synthetic. **Pigskin** can also refer to <u>football</u> generically.

*Man 1: Let's go outside and toss around the **pigskin**.*
Man 2: I'd rather toss around a Frisbee, I can't catch a football!

play ball (v) ○ At the beginning of a baseball game, the umpire announces "Let's **play ball**," which simply means "let's play the game." This term can be used outside of sports to describe situations that involve two parties that must cooperate.

*I am negotiating to buy a car, but the dealer won't **play ball** and reduce the price, so I'm going to buy my car elsewhere.*

pump iron (v) ○ To lift weights is to **pump iron**. This refers to the metal weights used in weightlifting.

*Mike can help you move that piano. He does nothing but **pump iron** all day, so he's really strong.*

ref (n) ○ **Ref** is short for a referee, who has the job of making sure that game rules are adhered to.

My <u>*roommate*</u> *and her* <u>*boyfriend*</u> *have been fighting all night, and I've been like a **referee**, trying to smooth things over and keeping their battle from getting* <u>*out of hand*</u>*.*

riding the pine (v) ○ Someone who is <u>benched</u> is **riding the pine,** which derives from the bench players sit on, which can be made of wood.

*I missed two practices in a row, and now I'm **riding the pine** during this weekend's game, which stinks, because I hate it when I can't play!*

right off the bat (adv) ○ **Right off the bat** means "immediately" or "right away."

Right off the bat, *you must register for classes.*

roll with the punches (v) ○ When you make it through a tough time or try to minimize a troublesome situation, you **roll with the punches.** This phrase originated from boxing, in which a boxer **rolls with the punches,** or tries to make sure his or her opponent does not squarely land any blows.

*I know that losing your apartment and failing a class are difficult, but you just have to **roll with the punches**, and everything will turn out okay.*

run numbers (v) ○ To **run numbers** is to be a <u>bookie</u>.

*Scott got arrested last night! The gambling investigators found out he was **running numbers** for a large gambling operation!*

scrub (adj) ⟲ In sports, a **scrub** is an athlete new to a team, usually a freshman. This word is used in nonsports speak to describe someone who is entry level or not important.

*I'm not going out with that boy; he's a total **scrub**. I only date important guys.*

shredding (v) ⟲ **Shredding** is a term used in snowboarding and surfing that means "to cut through" snow or water.

*Alan is an awesome snowboarder! He really **shredded** that course today!*

slam dunk (n) ⟲ This is a shot in basketball in which the player jumps off the ground and slams the ball into the net. Not every player can dunk, and it is quite an intimidating shot. This term is used outside of basketball to denote a good outcome, much like the term home run.

*Wow! Kevin's idea for a birthday party for his girlfriend was a **slam dunk**! She absolutely loved it!*

slugfest (n) ⟲ In baseball, a **slugfest** is when both teams are getting a lot of hits and scoring a lot of runs (sometimes a baseball game has very few hits). In nonbaseball use, **slugfest** indicates a big argument.

*My professor got into a virtual **slugfest** with the visiting professor who was observing our class. They were fighting about politics, and I thought they would get into an actual physical fight!*

slump (n) ◯ This term derives from baseball and indicates a player who has not gotten a hit in a long time. **Slump** can be used to describe any situation in which someone is not doing well and continues to do poorly.

*I'm in such a **slump** with my classes. I can't seem to get a good grade on any exam, and it's been going on all semester!*

snowboarding (v) ◯ This is a sport that involves a person "surfing" on snow on a board affixed to that person's feet. **Snowboarding** combines techniques from skiing, surfing, and skateboarding.

*Tracy is a great **snowboarder**! She was really <u>shredding</u> the mountain this morning.*

step up to the plate (v) ◯ To **step up to the plate** is to do something good in times of trouble; for example, a man who pulls someone from a burning car has **stepped up to the plate** by having the courage to do something and act on it. This derives from a batter in baseball literally walking up to home plate to bat.

*Jess really **stepped up to the plate** by volunteering to present our project in class, especially because she is afraid of speaking in public.*

strike out (v) ◯ In baseball, a batter is out when he or she gets three strikes. Three strikeouts results in the end of an inning. In common use, if you **strike out,** you fail.

Woman 1: Did that cute guy agree to go out with you?

*Woman 2: No, I **struck out**! He says he has a <u>girlfriend</u> already!*

tailgate (v, n) ○ To **tailgate** is to have a party with BBQ, other types of food, and drinks outdoors in the parking lot at a sporting event, usually football. The actual party itself is called a **tailgate.** Many people will arrive at the stadium hours before the game starts to eat and have a good time.

*Wow, this is the biggest **tailgate** party I've ever been to! There must be fifty fans here, and there is enough food for about 100 people!*

take a dive (v) ○ This term derives from boxing, in which a boxer who intentionally loses by pretending to be knocked out by his or her opponent **takes a dive.**

*Because I get higher grades on my exams than the rest of the class, my grade determines the curve. My roommate says she needs a bigger curve, so I **took a dive** on the last exam and did much worse than I usually do so the class would have a bigger curve.*

team player (n) ○ A **team player** is someone who gets along well with team members and, most importantly, puts the needs of the team ahead of his or her own needs.

*Bethany is really a **team player**. She canceled plans for Saturday night because that's the only night our study group can meet, and we all need to be present for our group to receive class credit.*

ump (n) ○ An **ump** is short for umpire, an official in the game of baseball. **Umps** make sure that the players follow the rules and that the game is played fairly. You will most likely hear **ump** only referring to baseball, although the long form, umpire, can be used in the same way as ref.

*The **ump** must be crazy! That was definitely a strike!*

ups (adj) ᴑ Someone who has **ups** can jump off the ground very high vertically. This term is usually applied to basketball players but can be used to describe anyone with the ability to jump high off the ground.

Man 1: Can you <u>slam dunk</u> a basketball?

Man 2: No, I don't have **ups** *like that. If I did, I'd play professional basketball!*

whiff (v) ᴑ When a batter gets a strike by failing to make contact with the ball, it's called a **whiff.** This term is often applied to any kind of mistake someone makes where he or she completely miss something or fail at something.

Man 1: I asked out Margie last night.

Man 2: How did that go?

Man 1: I totally **whiffed**! *She likes someone else, but she said she'd never go out with me anyway.*

whole nine yards (adv) ᴑ To go the **whole nine yards** means to complete something that you put a lot of work into. The **whole nine yards** can also mean something that is completed with no detail overlooked. The origin of this phrase is not known, and there is much debate as to where it came from, but we've included it in this chapter because most people identify this term as relating to sports.

She really went the **whole nine yards** *in planning this party. Every detail is perfect!*

wild card (n) ↺ (Quite a few sports have **wild-card** spots in their playoffs. We're using <u>football</u> to demonstrate.) A team that makes the National Football League (NFL) playoffs by having one of the two best records among nondivision winners in its conference is a **wild-card** team. (For more information on the playoff structure of the NFL, go to www.nfl.com.) In common use, **wild card** can mean anyone who makes the finals of something or wins something who was not expected to win.

*I can't believe he's taking Penny to the dance! She's such a **wild-card** choice. I can think of at least five other girls I thought he would take to the dance before he asked Penny!*

11

Join the Club—Greek Speak

What do we mean by "Greek" speak? Well, Greek refers to the Greek system, which is the system of fraternities (brotherhoods consisting of all-male members) and sororities (sisterhoods consisting of all-female members) on a college campus. Sororities and fraternities are named with a combination of Greek letters, usually three but sometimes two, that associate them with a national fraternity or sorority. Fraternities and sororities often have houses on campus where members live and meals are provided. There are many social activities associated with the Greek system, and if you find that a sorority or fraternity is right for you, it's a great situation in which to meet people. In this chapter, you will find words associated with the Greek system. The words in this chapter are not conventionally slang, but they are specialized college words you need to know if you want to participate in the Greek system.

bid (n) ☺ A **bid** is an invitation from a fraternity or sorority to join the club. You receive a bid after you have rushed and pledged.

> *Yay! I got a **bid** today from Sigma Sigma Sigma! All my hard work during the pledge period really paid off! I'll be a sister for life!*

big brother, big sister (n) ○ During your <u>pledge</u> period, you are paired with an existing member of the <u>house</u> who acts as a guide and a friend. These members are called **big brothers** and **big sisters**, which conveys a feeling of family. A **big brother** and **big sister** (often shortened as big bro and big sis) treat their *little brother* or *little sister* as one would treat and guide a younger sibling.

*My **big brother** has shown me how to act in the <u>house</u> and has taught me many things. He's really made my <u>pledge</u> period <u>awesome</u> and has shown me how to be a good member of the <u>house</u>.*

brothers (n) ○ The men who are full members of a fraternity are called **brothers.** To become a **brother**, you must complete a <u>pledge</u> period and be <u>inducted</u> into the <u>house</u>.

*Those fraternity **brothers** are so close to each other and always seem to be having fun—maybe because they live in the same <u>house</u>!*

chapter (n) ○ A **chapter** is a <u>house</u> on one particular college campus. A chapter is part of a <u>national</u> fraternity or sorority of the same name as the **chapter**. Each national fraternity or sorority is composed of individual **chapters** on individual campuses. A <u>brother</u> or <u>sister</u> is welcome at the **chapter** of his or her own fraternity or sorority on any other campus that member might visit or transfer to.

*I'm a member of the University of Wisconsin Alpha Alpha Alpha **chapter**. I went to visit the University of Alaska, and I was able to stay and party with the <u>sisters</u> of the Alaska **chapter**.*

dues (n) ○ Members of fraternities and sororities must pay **dues,** which are fees paid to the <u>house</u> to help pay for things such as food, maintenance, and parties, among other costs.

*I have to scrape together some money for the <u>house</u> **dues** to be eligible for social functions.*

formal (n) ○ A **formal** is a party given by the members and for the members of a fraternity or sorority. The party is usually in a banquet hall, and the members and their guests dress in <u>black-tie</u> attire. There is usually one **formal** in the spring and one in the fall, but this may vary.

*Jane bought the prettiest dress for the spring **formal**—it's at a really nice place and her date is a real <u>cutie</u>!*

frat, frats, frat boys (n) ○ Non-Greek students often refer to fraternities as **frats** and their members as **frat boys.** This can be interpreted as derogatory; and many fraternity members do not like the shortening of the name to **frats**.

***Frat boys** party too much.*

Greeks (n) ○ Members of the Greek system are often referred to as **Greeks.**

Man 1: Is your roommate a Greek?

Man 2: No, he's an <u>independent</u>.

Greek Week (n) ○ This is a week on campus in which all of the fraternities and sororities at a school compete in a series of games for which they are awarded points. Traditionally, each fraternity <u>house</u> pairs with a sorority <u>house</u>, and they compete together in the events and share the prize. The pairing that collects the most points becomes the **Greek Week** winner. Depending on the school, there may be awards or parties for the winner.

The <u>brothers</u> of Gamma Gamma Gamma and the <u>sisters</u> of Alpha Alpha Alpha paired together for **Greek Week.** *Their win in the volleyball tournament gave them enough points to be the* **Greek Week** *winners.*

hazing (v) ○ This is the practice of making <u>pledges</u> perform stunts, forcing them to drink, or making their life a <u>living hell</u> during the <u>pledge</u> period. **Hazing** is currently *outlawed* on all American college campuses and is considered cruel and dangerous.

Boy, the pledges really got **hazed** *last night. The <u>brothers</u> had a huge party and made the pledges clean the whole house afterward with toothbrushes!*

house (n) ○ The actual house in which the fraternity members or sorority members live is referred to as the fraternity **house** or sorority **house**, or often, simply "the **house**."

Do you need to go back to **the house** *to get your books for physics?*

house (n) ○ The actual fraternity or sorority is also referred to as the **house**.

I want to pledge Upsilon Upsilon Upsilon because it's such a great **house.**

house mom, house dad (n) ◯ A **house mom** is an older woman who lives in a sorority <u>house</u> and takes care of the members. A **house dad** is an older man who lives in a fraternity <u>house</u> and takes care of the members. This sometimes means keeping the members out of trouble!

*Our **house mom** is such a <u>bummer</u>. She caught us sneaking into the house after hours and punished us by making us do dishes for three days in a row!*

independent, indie (n) ◯ An **independent** is a college student who is not a member of the Greek system.

*My <u>roommate</u> hates sororities! She said she'd rather be an **independent** than <u>rush</u> a sorority.*

induction (n) ◯ An **induction** is the ceremony in which <u>pledges</u> are welcomed into the <u>house</u> and become full <u>brothers</u> or <u>sisters</u>. **Induction** ceremonies are secret and known only to members of the <u>house</u>.

*I was **inducted** into Sigma Sigma Sigma last night; I'm a <u>sister</u> now.*

invite (n) ◯ When someone has completed the <u>rush</u> period, he or she will receive an **invite** to <u>pledge</u> a fraternity or sorority and have to choose whether to accept or reject the **invite**. A person can receive an invite to more than one <u>house</u>, but he or she can only choose one at which to <u>pledge</u>.

*I got my **invite** to <u>pledge</u> Alpha Alpha Alpha, and I'm so <u>psyched</u>! It's the best sorority on campus.*

lavaliere (n) ○ A **lavaliere** is a charm for a necklace that has the letters of the fraternity or sorority on it and sometimes a <u>chapter</u> symbol or crest. A fraternity member may give his <u>girlfriend</u> his **lavaliere** to indicate a serious commitment but may be the subject of relentless teasing by his <u>brothers</u>.

*I gave my girlfriend my **lavaliere** on Valentine's Day. She said it's the most romantic thing I've ever done.*

legacy (n) ○ A **legacy** is a <u>pledge</u> who has a mother, father, or other close family member who was a member of the fraternity or sorority being pledged. **Legacies** must <u>pledge</u>, but are almost always admitted to the <u>house</u>.

*My dad was a member of Omega Omega Omega, so I'm a **legacy**, which means it will be a <u>piece of cake</u> to get in.*

letters (n) ○ The Greek letters that make up the name of the <u>house</u> are called, simply, **letters.** The **letters** are often displayed on clothing, jewelry, and <u>bumper stickers</u>. They are considered sacred and are not supposed to be worn by anyone who is not a member of the fraternity or sorority.

*My <u>roommate</u> is an <u>indie</u>, and she borrowed my sweatshirt with my **letters** on it. Wow, did I get <u>reamed out</u> by the president.*

national (n) ○ This refers to the national organization of which each <u>house</u> is a <u>chapter</u>. One of the <u>perks</u> of being in the Greek system is the default membership in the **national** organization. Members are members for life, and many connections can be made through the **national** fraternity or sorority.

*I went on a job interview yesterday, and the guy who interviewed me is an alumnus of my fraternity—he hired me on the spot! He said he always takes care of <u>brothers</u>, and he's on the board of the **national**!*

officers, executive board (n) ○ Each <u>house</u> has members who are elected **officers** who help run the <u>house</u>; as a group, they are the **executive board**. Usually, each <u>house</u> has a president, a vice president, a treasurer, a secretary, a steward (who takes care of the food), a <u>rush chairman</u>, and a <u>pledge master</u>. However, the **offices** vary from <u>house</u> to <u>house</u>, so one house may have a social chairman on the board, but another may not.

*The **officers** had a meeting last night and decided to have our <u>formal</u> on a boat, which <u>sucks</u>, because I get seasick.*

pledge (n) ○ A **pledge** is a person who has made it through the <u>rush</u> period and has been invited to pledge the <u>house</u>. The person then enters into the **pledge** period, which is a trial period, before becoming a full <u>brother</u> or <u>sister</u>. During this period, **pledges** learn about the fraternity or sorority history and all about current and past members.

*I made it through <u>rush</u>, and now I'm a Delta Delta Delta **pledge**. If I don't <u>screw up</u>, I'll be inducted as a <u>brother</u> at the end of the semester.*

pledge book (n) ○ A **pledge book** is a notebook that <u>pledges</u> are often required to keep. What is written in the book varies from <u>house</u> to <u>house</u> and between fraternities and sororities, but much of it is <u>house</u> history and information about current members of the <u>house</u> that the <u>pledges</u> collect as part of their learning period. The book is important and private—one should not lose a **pledge book**.

*I had to find out a funny story about Leigh, the <u>house</u> president, and record it in my **pledge book** as part of my <u>pledge</u> duties.*

pledge master (n) ꙩ The person in charge of the <u>pledge</u> period who is responsible for the <u>pledges</u> is called the **pledge master.** The **pledge master** makes sure the <u>pledges</u> are treated correctly by the <u>brothers</u> and <u>sisters</u> and handles any problems or disputes that may arise during the pledge period.

*Two of our <u>pledges</u> got into a fight with one of the <u>sisters</u> last night, and the **pledge master** had to <u>break it up</u>.*

pledge pin (n) ꙩ Each <u>pledge</u> is given a **pledge pin** during <u>pledge</u> period. Usually, the <u>pledge</u> is required to wear the pin at all times.

*My <u>big sister</u> caught me in the dining hall without my **pledge pin**—I'm in trouble now!*

rush chairman (n) ꙩ The **rush chairman** is in charge of the <u>rush week</u>. This can be a stressful position, because there are many people to manage as well as the rush events that must be planned.

*I'm **rush chairman**, and I've been running around like crazy trying to get the food and decorations coordinated. I really want the rushees to be impressed with our <u>house</u>.*

rush week (n) ꙩ This is the period when the fraternities and sororities on campus recruit new members. During **rush week**, students on campus can visit numerous fraternities or sororities to see if they are interested in joining any. **Rushing** works both ways: The <u>sisters</u> or <u>brothers</u> <u>check out</u> the rushees, but the rushees also check out the <u>house</u> members. Even if you do not think you want to join the Greek system, **rush week** can be a really great way to meet people, especially if you are a freshman or new to the country.

*My <u>roommate</u> dragged me out to **rush week**. I realized I didn't want to be in a sorority, but I met some really great people that week, both <u>Greeks</u> and <u>indies</u>.*

sisters (n) ◯ The women who are full members of a sorority are called **sisters.** To become a **sister**, or full member, you must complete a <u>pledge</u> period and be <u>inducted</u> into the <u>house</u>.

*Those sorority **sisters** are so close to each other and always seem to be having fun—maybe because they live in the same <u>house</u>.*

suicide (v) ◯ When a person (usually a girl) decides she only wants to <u>pledge</u> one <u>house</u>, she informs the other houses that she <u>rushed</u> that she only wants to be in one sorority, and won't join any other. In other words, if she can't be in the sorority she wants, she doesn't want to be <u>Greek</u>. It's called **suicide**, because the girl kills her chances at another sorority.

*I'm **suiciding.** I only want to join Sigma Sigma Sigma; I won't accept anything else.*

12

The Good, the Bad, and the Other

In this chapter, you will find words that denote good things, words that denote bad things, and other words—those that don't fit neatly into any category.

86 (it) (v) ⊃ To **86 it** is to delete or cancel something.

> *We **86'd** the party that was planned for tonight. There's too much snow for people to get here, so we'll reschedule for next week.*

ABCs (n) ⊃ The **ABCs** of something are the basics of something. This comes from the idea that children first learn the alphabet, the **ABCs,** before they learn to read—the alphabet is the basic part.

> *You need to learn the **ABCs** of good study habits before you can be a successful student.*

a living hell (adj) ◯ If something is **a living hell,** it is very bad.

> *My roommate makes life **a living hell!** She leaves old food and dirty*
> *dishes everywhere, and she borrows my clothes without asking and*
> *ruins them!*

all that (adj) ◯ Someone who is **all that** is a great person. This usually implies that a person is attractive, well-dressed, and generally appealing to others. This is a high compliment. (Also see page 97)

> *That girl is **all that!** She'd never date a loser like me.*

awesome (adj) ◯ The official dictionary definition is "something that inspires awe," and the word had a religious connotation in its original meaning. However, **awesome** has been adopted into common use (and you'll hear it all the time) to denote anything that is great or wonderful. A synonym is **killer.**

> *The concert last night was totally **awesome!** It's the best concert I've*
> *ever seen!*

bad taste in one's mouth (n) ◯ Something that is distasteful or unpleasant is said to leave a **bad taste in one's mouth** after the fact.

> *My experience with a really mean English professor left such a **bad***
> ***taste in my mouth** that I switched my major to political science!*

basket case (n) ◯ A person who is a **basket case** is crazy or having a moment of craziness due to extensive worry.

> *Her husband was a total **basket case** during the birth of their child. I've*
> *never seen anyone so nervous!*

bed of roses (n) ○ This phrase has a positive connotation. A **bed of roses** denotes a wonderful place; sometimes, it denotes something that is easy.

*My graduation party was a **bed of roses**. I've never had so much fun at a party before.*

big time (adj) ○ **Big time** means "major" and "important." A person can have a **big-time** job, a **big-time** crush on someone, do someone a **big-time** favor, or <u>screw up</u> **big time.**

*My brother is a **big-time** executive in an important company, so he makes a lot of money.*

bitter pill (n) ○ A **bitter pill** is something that is hard to accept.

*Failing out of school is a **bitter pill** to swallow, especially because you worked so hard to get good grades.*

black mark (n) ○ A **black mark** on someone's record is a bad incident or something negative someone has done in the past.

*Cheating on that final exam will leave a big **black mark** on your school record. All the business schools you are applying to will know what you did.*

boo-boo (n) ○ A **boo-boo** is a mistake or a social gaff.

*I made a **boo-boo** when I told my friend that her hair looked awful, because now she won't speak to me!*

boo-yah! (n) ○ **Boo-yah!** is an expression of delight that signifies an accomplishment.

Boo-yah! *I <u>aced</u> that final exam!*

buddy (n) ◯ A **buddy** is a friend.

> *My **buddies** and I went to an <u>awesome</u> party last night.*

bum rap (n) ◯ A **bum rap** is something that is unfair. A person who has been unfairly judged about something he or she has done has gotten a **bum rap.**

> *I really got a **bum rap** at the car dealership. I ended up paying way more than I should have because the salesperson took advantage of me.*

bum (something) (v) ◯ To **bum** something off of someone is to borrow something from that person, as in, "Can I **bum a pencil** from you?"

> *Woman 1: May I **bum that sweater** off you tonight?*
> *Woman 2: Yes, but give it back tomorrow.*

cabin fever (n) ◯ **Cabin fever** is what happens to people who are stuck inside in the same place for too long a time.

> *We haven't been able to leave the <u>dorm</u> for two days because of the snow! I have total **cabin fever** now, and I have to get out of here!*

cheesy (adj) ◯ **Cheesy** is a negative term that means something is flimsy, bad, cheap, or generally not good. When used to describe a person, **cheesy** is similar in meaning to <u>loser</u>.

> *My <u>roommate</u> likes the **cheeziest** things. She has the worst taste in clothes ever!*

chintzy (n) ◯ Something that is **chintzy** is poorly constructed.

> *This <u>dorm</u> couch is pretty **chintzy.** I'm worried it will collapse if too many people sit on it.*

cool (adj) ↻ Perhaps one of the most commonly used slang terms among the widest group of people, **cool** means "good." **Cool** can also serve as an affirmative statement in place of the word "yes."

>   Man: *Do you want to have dinner tomorrow with me?*
>
>   Woman: **Cool.**
>
>   Man: *Great! I'll meet you at your <u>lounge</u> at 8 p.m.*

cushy (adj) ↻ Something that is **cushy** is good and easy to do. This term often refers to a person's occupation (a **cushy** job) or lifestyle (a **cushy** life).

>   *She has the most **cushy** job ever! She gets paid a lot of money to sit behind a counter and greet people.*

dibs on (something) (n) ↻ If you have **dibs on** something, you have laid claim to it.

>   *I have first **dibs on that book** when you're done with it, so don't give it to anyone else.*

dicey (adj) ↻ A situation that is **dicey** is dangerous or uncomfortable.

>   *Jumping off that cliff is **dicey,** because if your parachute doesn't work, you could suffer a lot of injuries.*

fierce (adj) ↻ Something that is **fierce** is incredibly good or <u>hot</u>. This word falls into the slang category because its slang meaning is the opposite of the official dictionary definition, which implies that something is scary or dangerous and difficult.

>   *That guy is a **fierce** dresser. He may even be the best dressed guy on campus!*

fresh (adj) ○ Something that is **fresh** is <u>cool</u>. A synonym is **fly.**

> *Those sneakers are **fresh!** Where can I get a pair?*

get a life (v) ○ If someone tells you to **get a life,** that person is telling you to go away or that you are boring and need to find something to occupy your time.

> *You are such a <u>loser</u>!* ***Get a life!***

get reamed out (v) ○ To **get reamed out** is to get yelled at or to be reprimanded by someone for something that you did.

> *I got an F on my term paper, and my professor really **reamed me out!** He yelled at me for 10 minutes straight!*

give it a whirl (v) ○ **Give it a whirl** means "give something a try."

> *Woman: I don't know how to inline skate.*
>
> *Man: Why don't you rent some skates and **give it a whirl**? It's really fun.*

glitch (n) ○ A **glitch** is something that goes wrong or that causes something to fail.

> *A **glitch** in the grading system on campus resulted in all students receiving an A in every class on their report cards. It will take weeks to fix it and send out forms with students' correct grades on them.*

glitzy (adj) ○ **Glitzy** means fancy or flashy and implies that something or someone is worth a lot of money.

> *This hotel is so **glitzy**. Everything is made of marble, and there are crystal chandeliers and gold accents everywhere.*

gross (adj) ○ Something that is **gross** is highly unappetizing or nauseating.

*Picking your nose is so **gross!***

had it up to here (v) ○ Saying you've **had it up to here** with a situation implies that the situation is bad and you have reached your breaking point.

*I've **had it up to here** with my messy <u>roommate</u>. If he throws one more dirty towel on the floor, there's going to be a <u>slugfest</u>!*

hairy situation (n) ○ A **hairy situation** is a precarious, or risky, situation that can go wrong at any minute. A synonym is "**in a jam**."

*Dating your <u>roommate's</u> <u>boyfriend</u> is a really **hairy situation**. You'll be in so much trouble if she finds out.*

hatin' life (v) ○ If you are **hatin' life,** you are miserable. This usually implies a temporarily bad time, not an ongoing situaion.

*I'm working full-time, and I have a full courseload this semester, so I'm really **hatin' life** right now. Next semester will be better, though.*

hit (v) ○ To **hit** something is to go to a place or go somewhere.

*Let's **hit** Sal's Pizza on the way home. I'm starving.*

hot (adj) ○ **Hot** means popular or excellent when used to describe a place. When used to describe a person, it means "very attractive."

*The new restaurant on campus is so **hot** right now that you need to wait three weeks to get a reservation for a table.*

huh? (n) ○ **Huh?** means "what?" and can stand on its own as a sentence. People usually say **huh?** when they don't hear something and need it repeated.

> *Man 1: Wake up! It's time for class.*
>
> *Man 2:* ***Huh?***
>
> *Man 1: I said wake up!*

icky (adj) ○ **Icky** means gross, nauseating, or distasteful.

> *The shower in the <u>dorm</u> is so* ***icky!*** *There is so much mildew that the walls are green instead of white.*

ins and outs (n) ○ To know the **ins and outs** of something is to know it very well.

> *I've been a student here for seven years, so no one else knows the* ***ins and outs*** *of this campus like I do.*

keep it real (v) ○ To **keep it real** is to be down to earth, or realistic, and to not have an attitude about the good things you have.

> *You should* ***keep it real*** *and act just like you did before you won the lottery.*

mad about (adv) ○ To be **mad about** something is to like that thing a lot or to love it.

> *I'm* ***mad about*** *<u>football</u>. It's my favorite sport in the world.*

out of hand (adv) ○ When a situation is **out of hand,** it is out of control or chaotic.

> *The situation with my <u>roommate</u> is completely* ***out of hand.*** *She steals all my clothes and is not even nice to me!*

perk (n) ○ A **perk** is an added benefit or an incentive for doing something.

> *One of the **perks** of being an <u>RA</u> is that you get free room and board from the school.*

phat (adj) ○ **Phat** means "very good" or "very cool."

> *That's a **phat** movie. I want to see it again!*

piece of cake (adj) ○ Something that is a **piece of cake** is extraordinarily easy.

> *My classes are a **piece of cake** this semester. I should get <u>easy A's</u> for sure.*

plan B (n) ○ **Plan B** is a generic reference to an alternate plan to the main plan, plan A.

> *Plan A is to go to all three big parties tonight. **Plan B** is to only go to one party but to have a lot of fun there.*

pretty (adj) ○ The dictionary definition of **pretty** is "attractive." However, the word **pretty** is also used to mean "very" or "a lot of."

> *That girl is **pretty** mean. She's always insulting other people.*

psyched (adv) ○ **Psyched** means "excited."

> *I'm **psyched** for my trip to Mexico for <u>spring break</u>.*

random (adj) ○ Random denotes an unusual or unexpected situation.

> *Last night was so **random**. I ended up at a party full of people I didn't know because I ran into some **random** boy I usually never see, and he invited me.*

rank on (v) ○ To **rank on** someone is to make fun of or tease that person. A synonym is **tool on.**

*My friends are really **ranking on** me for taking ballet class. They think ballet is not for boys.*

riot (adj) ○ Something that is a **riot** is extremely funny.

*My professor is such a **riot.** She tells so many jokes that most of class is spent laughing.*

screw up (v) ○ To **screw up** is to make a mistake.

*I really **screwed up** the butter cookies I was baking—I used margarine instead of butter.*

sketchy (adj) ○ **Sketchy** describes an untrustworthy or potentially dangerous situation or person. A person who is nervous about something is **sketched out.**

*This place it **sketchy.** Let's get out of here.*

snag (v) ○ To **snag** something is to take something without permission.

*I **snagged** two extra desserts from the dining hall, so my <u>roommate</u> and I will have a snack for later.*

space (v) ○ To **space** is to forget something.

Man 1: Did you do your part of the science project?

*Man 2: I'm really sorry, but I **spaced.** I can have it ready tomorrow.*

sucks (v) ○ Something that **sucks** is terrible or distasteful.

*My morning class **sucks!** The professor is really boring and mean!*

take (something) **with a grain of salt** (v) ○ **Take something with a grain of salt** means "don't believe everything someone tells you without being skeptical."

*I would **take** Mike's advice **with a grain of salt** if I were you. He makes a lot of bad decisions.*

whatever (adv) ○ In slang usage, **whatever** means "I don't care."

Woman: What do you want to do tonight?

*Man: **Whatever.***

wicked (adj) ○ **Wicked** means "<u>cool</u>," but unlike the word "cool," **wicked** is a common expression in specific regional areas: New England and Mid-Atlantic states.

*That boy is **wicked!***

your bag (n) ○ **Your bag** means "what you are interested in."

*I don't like pink hair, but if that's **your bag,** go ahead and dye your hair.*

zoned out (v) ○ People who are **zoned out** are not paying attention to what is going on around them and are "staring into space."

*I was so **zoned out** from lack of sleep that I almost got hit by a car because I crossed the road at the wrong time.*

Index

D

About the Author

Jamie Drucker graduated from the University of Maryland and is currently a graduate student in education. She currently teaches language arts, public speaking, and drama at the high school level. She lives in New Jersey with her Labrador retriever and Yorkshire terrier.